STF.

You can return this item to any library but please note that not all libraries are open every day.
Items must be returned on or before the due date. Failure to do so will result in overdue charges.
Items may be renewed unless requested by another customer, in person or by telephone, on two occasions only. Your membership card number will be required.
Please look after this item – you may be charged for any damage.

Headquarters:
Information, Culture & Community Learning,
Town Hall, Bournemouth BH2 6DY

BOUF

D1342854

Making the Most of RFID in Libraries

Making the Most of RFID in Libraries

Martin Palmer

facet publishing

Published by
Facet Publishing
7 Ridgmount Street
London WC1E 7AE
www.facetpublishing.co.uk

Facet Publishing is wholly owned by
CILIP: the Chartered Institute of Library
and Information Professionals.

PEFC

PEFC/16-33-111

CATG-PEFC-052

www.pefc.org

Text printed on PEFC accredited material. The
policy of Facet Publishing is to use papers that
are natural, renewable and recyclable products,
made from wood grown in sustainable forests.
In the manufacturing process of our books,
and to further our policy, preference is given to
printers that have FSC and PEFC Chain of
Custody certification. The FSC and/or PEFC
logos will appear on those books where full
certification has been granted to the printer
concerned.

*British Library Cataloguing in Publication
Data*
A catalogue record for this book is
available from the British Library.

ISBN 978-1-85604-634-3

First published 2009

Typeset from author's disk in 11/15 pt
University Old Style and Zurich by Facet
Publishing.
Printed and made in Great Britain by
MPG Books Ltd, Bodmin, Cornwall.

Contents

Contents

Preface

Introduction

Radio Frequency Identification (RFID) is no longer quite the latest thing on the block - at least as far as libraries are concerned. However, although RFID is being adopted by libraries around the world at a very rapid rate, it is a dynamic technology whose future development is impossible to predict.

For the manager considering RFID, whether as a solution to a library's problems or as an opportunity to rethink service delivery, this presents both an opportunity and a challenge - the technology appears to provide a number of benefits (why else would there be such a rush to install it?), but it takes so many different forms that it is difficult to discern which may prove to be the Betamax versions - technologically sound but commercial failures - five years down the line, resulting in a potentially distressing waste of time and money.

The simple fact is that - for any library management that is only slightly risk averse - RFID is still not the path to take. There are so many imponderables - choice of system, choice of frequency, choice of tag, tag deployment method, and much more - that anybody looking for a future-proofed investment is going to be disappointed and should postpone their decision for a while.

Consequently, this book does not claim to offer a guide to choosing the definitive RFID system, nor does it go very deeply into the technology itself. It does, however, outline the main elements to be considered when choosing a system, both for RFID and for existing procedures and practices. By providing a general introduction to the topic, describing the different approaches that have been taken to using RFID in libraries and outlining the pros and cons of each, it outlines the benefits that can result from RFID adoption, illustrating why – despite the possible problems – it has proved to be so popular with so many libraries in such a short time, and explores its potential for application to other aspects of library work in the future.

The essential aims of this book, then, are to help library managers decide whether RFID has anything to offer them and – if so – how to make the most of the benefits while mitigating the risks inherent in adopting this rapidly developing technology.

Terminology: a note about 'customers'

Much of the emphasis of this book is about improving the experience of the library user and it draws on some retail techniques which fall under the generic term 'customer care'. It is generally accepted that library users have a relationship with their library that is both more complicated and more rewarding than that between a customer and a shop, as their position as citizens or students gives them fundamentally different rights and expectations as stakeholders. However, the term 'customer' is used throughout this book for the sake of simplicity.

Acknowledgements

Thanks are due to many current and former colleagues who have been part of my involvement in RFID. From Essex County Council's Libraries Department past and present these include, among many others: Michele Jones, Geoff Elgar, Gaynor Bell, Nicola Baker, Jenny Glayzer and Deborah Raddon. From Book Industry Communication (BIC) and EDItEUR, Brian Green and Peter Kilborn. All members of the BIC/CILIP RFID in Libraries Group, the E4Libraries Committee, and the ISO Working Group on RFID in Libraries, including Simon Edwards and Mick Fortune, and to Paul Chartier of Praxis Consultants.

For her help and advice on retail techniques, thanks to Fiona Emberton of John Stanley Associates and Embervision.

Thanks also to Helen Carley at Facet Publishing for her help and encouragement in developing the ideas for this book.

Finally, thanks to Marjorie, Amie and Rebecca for their patience . . .

Chapter 1

RFID, libraries and the wider world

> New to RFID? Curious about how it works? Want to know about RFID in the wider world? This chapter looks at the history and background of RFID technology, and outlines some of its uses in everyday life as well as exploring its main applications in libraries.

Why RFID and libraries?

Few, if any, technologies have had as immediate an impact on libraries as that of Radio Frequency Identification (RFID). From a standing start in the mid 1990s to a position where an estimated 300 sites worldwide were home to 120 million tagged items by 2005, RFID has spread rapidly around the world's libraries seemingly with little to slow its progress.

This would be impressive under any circumstances, but it has been achieved against a background in which, even now, most industries still see RFID as an experimental product, whose return on investment is doubtful. The majority of commercial applications remain restricted to limited aspects of supply chain management, with tags used at the consignment or pallet level rather than on individual items.

At the time of writing, the very few commercial organizations operating RFID at item level on any significant scale are still seen very much as pioneers, with the RFID industry still some distance from even beginning to approach critical mass for item-level adoption.

Consequently, the claim in 2004 that 'libraries are much further along with using RFID in a consumer environment than anybody else' (Lichtenberg, 2004) might have been surprising, but could easily be justified. The main reasons for this are that, for many library managers:

- RFID is ideally suited to library applications; the need to keep track of thousands of individual items involved in millions of transactions in the most efficient way possible is only one of many applications to which RFID is very well suited.
- Additionally, however, RFID has a major advantage over other technologies used in libraries for this purpose: the tag has the ability to combine the functions of a barcode (as a unique item identifier) and a security device (able to indicate that an item is being removed from the library without permission). This by itself would be attractive, but, with the added benefits of the ability to read multiple items and to do this virtually simultaneously without the need for line of sight, RFID clearly has a lot to interest any librarian looking to streamline operations.

Perhaps the reason why people not involved in libraries express surprise at finding them at the forefront of adopting item-level RFID tagging is a perception that libraries are highly risk averse, resistant to both change and the application of technology. However, library managers, having experienced developments since the late 1960s, from manual Browne-type systems, using pieces of cardboard, through to photo-charging, offline disk-based data capture and proprietary online 'integrated library systems', to web-based modular approaches would probably beg to differ.

In fact – being very venerable institutions – libraries have a longer history than most of using technology to adapt both to their changing environments and to the media they provide for their users. Whether coping with the change from papyrus roll to vellum codex or from paper to electronic media, libraries have an excellent record over the centuries of responding to these demands by changing their mode of organization, adopting different approaches to security, and adapting the ways in which their collections can be accessed.

This openness to new ways of working in order to improve the reader's experience perhaps goes some way to explaining the rapid growth in RFID take-up in libraries. RFID not only offers another opportunity to redefine service delivery, but, according to some commentators, has the potential to revolutionize library processes to a greater extent than anything before it.

RFID – the technology: a brief history

The history of RFID is surprisingly contentious, although there is general agreement that the basic technology dates back to at least the Second World War. At that time, the constituent processes of RFID – a transponder, reacting to a signal received by a transmitter, either reflects the signal back or broadcasts one of its own – were used to enable swift differentiation between friendly and enemy aircraft.

However, it was only in 1973 that Mario W. Cardullo received a patent (US Patent 3,713,148) for what is now clearly recognizable as a passive, read-write RFID tag. His description of the development of the concept (Cardullo, n.d.) makes it clear that the idea was to converge different but related existing technologies – the 'friend or foe' aircraft detector system described above, electronic security systems, and a chip with memory capacity – into a smaller and portable format.

This format – the tag – would later become available in a variety of shapes and sizes (some being smaller than a grain of rice, others more like a book in size and weight) but the essential content would almost always consist of two main elements – a memory chip and an antenna, usually made from copper or aluminium – bound together into a single device.

First commercial applications

The patent application also described some of the potential uses for the device, including what was to become one of its earliest and most ubiquitous commercial applications – automated toll payment – which has been a common feature on bridges, tunnels and motorways since the mid 1980s. This, in turn, appears to have been a further development of one of RFID's earliest deployments (like most, emanating originally from the defence industry), which was the tracking of nuclear materials at Los Alamos National Laboratory in the US.

Other commercial applications soon followed, including security cards for controlling access to buildings, the tagging of cattle, and – perhaps most commonly – logistics solutions, particularly the tracking of reusable containers such as beer kegs, which are often both expensive to produce and extremely attractive to a wide range of users outside the supply chain. In contrast, RFID's visibility in everyday life at item level has been fairly limited until comparatively recently, with most common commercial uses of RFID still remaining at the pallet or consignment level in warehousing and transport applications.

The usual explanation given for this comparatively slow commercial take-up of RFID at item level is the relatively high cost of a tag compared with that of a more popular competing device – the barcode. However, accurate comparison of the benefits and disadvantages of RFID to those of barcodes is not always easy, and tends to concentrate on the relative pricing of the tag and the barcode alone, rather than on the costs and benefits of the technologies as a whole.

RFID or barcodes?

Such comparisons also tend to emphasize the advantages enjoyed by the barcode resulting from its early widespread adoption, and as a result – in libraries, as elsewhere – the RFID tag has tended to be seen as a modern usurper of the barcode's role. However, they are much more closely contemporaneous than might first be thought, with barcodes not being commercially available until 1966, while the first instance of a supermarket scanning a barcode (on a packet of chewing gum) did not occur until 1974.

So, the ubiquity of the barcode rather than the RFID tag in everyday applications is not really attributable simply to its having been around longer. Rather, it is partly to do with a perception of RFID's higher cost and the early application (or otherwise, in the case of RFID) of standards. As we shall see throughout this book, these themes recur again and again in the story of the use of RFID in libraries and elsewhere.

RFID – the technology: frequencies

Rather than describing a single entity, RFID is really a shorthand term for a range of technologies which share the same basic physics and components as described in the Second World War application referred to earlier. However, this can be misleading, as RFID is employed at a number of different frequencies and tags can be either active (containing their own battery) or passive (finding their energy from the scanning antenna). The longevity of active tags is effectively determined by the durability of the battery on which they rely (unless it can be easily replaced or recharged), while passive tags clearly do not have such a dependency – although there may be environmental constraints or weaknesses in their construction that may affect their effectiveness over time.

In addition to all of these variations between tags themselves, their readability will also vary considerably according the scanner being used. The power and versatility of these devices is increasing at a rapid pace, and often the source of improvements in RFID systems is the scanner rather than the tag.

These differences are particularly important, as RFID's behaviour and potential applications vary accordingly, and this needs to be borne in mind when discussing both the advantages and problems of using it. RFID is also a technology that is developing all the time, and some things thought impossible only a few years ago are now available as part of functioning systems.

It is, then, a very complicated area, but the main categories, comprising four broad frequency groupings, are described below.

Low Frequency (LF) (up to 148 kHz)

This is used mainly for access control and animal identification, and is particularly well suited to use in hostile environments – the cost of these tags varies considerably according to the conditions in which they are intended to work. This frequency has the advantage of having a high penetration of liquids, and can also be used around metal with some success – although no RFID tag is able to read through metal. It is usually readable up to a distance of 10 cm, but some tags can be read from a greater distance. This frequency was used for the first major applications of RFID in the 1980s.

High Frequency (HF) (13.56 MHz)

This is the frequency used by the great majority of RFID libraries, and is also used for smart cards, access control and vehicle immobilization. It has medium penetration of liquids, but does not work well with metals, and is usually readable up to a distance of one metre. Development of this frequency was prompted by the need for a tag that could be used in very large quantities at a comparatively low cost, and it began to be adopted extensively during the 1990s.

Ultra High Frequency (UHF) (433 MHz and beyond)

Originally used mainly for pallets, UHF is now increasingly used for item-level tagging. It has the advantage of working well around metals but has low penetration of liquids. This limitation is fairly crucial from a library point of view when one remembers that the human body is predominantly composed of water, thus making tags fairly easy to mask. However, the recent development of 'near field' UHF has reduced the effect of this limitation. Read distances can be up to 100 m with active tags, although with passive tags this reduces to less than 10 m. Common applications of tags at 433 MHz include the remote locking of cars and their (often controversial) use by local authorities in refuse collection, where tags are placed in domestic wheeled bins to identify the property using them.

Microwave (2.45 GHz)

This is used mainly by Wi-Fi and Bluetooth applications. All low and high frequency tags are passive, while, as indicated above, UHF tags may be passive or active. To complicate things yet further, some tags can be semi-passive – containing an on-board power source but not communicating actively. Also, there are various options that can make tags operate and behave differently, such as on-tag memory, functionality and sensors. To provide an indication of the range of sophistication involved, not only can on-tag memory be Read Only, Write Once Read Many, or

Read-Write, with some elements being lockable – but also all of these elements can be present in the same tag.

A simple guide to all of this is that, generally speaking, the smaller the tag the shorter the read range; the lower the frequency, the shorter the read range; and that passive tags have a shorter read range than active tags, as they have no power of their own.

Until recently, all library applications were HF (13.56 MHz), but, as previously mentioned, developments in UHF technology have meant that it is now possible to use it more successfully in a library context. As a result, some UHF installations have now been undertaken in libraries in Australia and Japan (where it has been proposed that UHF should be the standard for libraries in the near future), and they also form the basis of the system adopted by the Selexyz bookshop chain in the Netherlands.

RFID – the technology: process

Regardless of frequency and active or passive status, the basic process involved in all RFID transactions is the same: a scanning device detects a radio frequency (RF) signal from a transponder – the tag.

Unfortunately, it seems likely that this shared basic process, which has led to the adoption of RFID as a shorthand term for what is actually a range of differently performing technologies, is the source of much of the concern about its potential for enabling the invasion of privacy in some parts of the world – if tags can be used to track the movement of cattle, then why not human beings?

One of the rare appearances of RFID in the mainstream media to date, a TV advert for IBM (see http://uk.youtube.com/watch?v=oAvQcYcvyaw) showing a secretary at a desk in the middle of a desert road, informing two truck drivers that she knew they were lost because 'the boxes told her', further suggests to the layman that concern about the use of what appears to be the same technology in libraries may not be entirely misplaced. These anxieties are explored further in Chapter 5.

RFID – a disruptive technology . . .?

RFID is frequently referred to as a 'disruptive' technology. This is a term that is used quite widely to cover innovations in general, but it also has a more specific meaning. Clayton Christensen (1997) developed this particular interpretation of the phrase, and although he later amended his description to 'disruptive innovation', recognizing that technology by itself is unable to change anything, it is the original term that has endured. According to Christensen's analysis, some technologies are so radically different from everything else currently available that they either overturn the existing dominant technology in the market or simply create a new market altogether. They contrast with 'sustaining' technologies, which tend to be incremental and are designed to improve existing mainstream products.

Examples of this kind of fundamental shift in everyday life include the change from the horse-drawn carriage to the internal combustion engine; from film to digital photography; and from printing to desk-top publishing. A brief look at some applications for RFID in the world outside libraries certainly suggests that it has the potential to fulfil most of the criteria of a disruptive technology. Although still in its infancy in retail applications, some of the scenarios made possible by linking 'smart' tags to similarly 'smart' domestic goods show how RFID can provide benefits not only in the early phases of the supply chain but also to the end user – the consumer.

For example, the advantages to retailers provided by tagging perishable goods are not too difficult to envisage – more accurate stock control, automatic reordering, and so on. However, if the customer buying the goods possesses a refrigerator with an appropriate scanner – a 'smart fridge' – then they can benefit from a number of potential value-added features. Some of these are simply pragmatic – such as alerts to when the goods have has passed their sell-by date, thus avoiding the possibility of exposure to food poisoning or worse.

More imaginatively, however, the 'smart fridge' could also analyse its own contents and provide recipes or suggestions for meals based on them. Building on that concept, shoppers in possession of a suitably enabled mobile phone could dial their smart fridges from the supermarket, and, having checked the contents, make their purchases in a more purposive manner. Both Samsung and Electrolux have demonstrated that such applications are workable, although it seems doubtful that they can be produced cost-effectively at present (Batista, 2003a).

RFID and the wider world – some existing applications

The use of RFID tags is already quite widespread in some elements of the production of cars and electronic goods, but it could also potentially support servicing and maintenance throughout a product's life, providing mechanics and repair men with a detailed history of any work that has been carried out previously, including replacement of parts.

Some very simple applications of RFID in day-to-day household products are beginning to appear, such as domestic heaters with detachable RFID thermostats. These heaters can be regulated according to the temperature in any part of the house, rather than only that of their actual location. Similarly, RFID-enabled doorbells mean that the placing of the sounder unit can be completely independent of the door, anywhere in the building, without the need for extensive cabling.

Leisure uses

The world of sport offers some of the most inventive uses of RFID – the tag in a 'smart' golf ball means that it need never be lost; tagged sports shoes enable much more accurate timings in athletics events; while tagged footballs may finally result in definitive refereeing decisions in 'did the ball cross the line?' situations.

The use of RFID in ticketing of major sports events has not only become an effective hindrance to counterfeiters but has also provided organizers with the facility to manage large crowds more effectively on the day. In the UK Manchester City, Fulham and Reading are just some of the Premiership football teams to use RFID tickets to reduce queues and increase safety (McCue, 2006), while much of the efficiency of the Beijing Olympic Games stemmed from its use of RFID in a wide range of behind-the-scenes applications.

Alton Towers theme park in the UK offers visitors the facility to wear an RFID-enabled wristband to create a DVD of their day at the park. The 'Your Day' wristband triggers cameras located around the venue and on the rides to create 'a unique personalized movie' to take home at the end of the visit.

Animals and people

However, alongside these comparatively benign applications there are some intrusive, and sometimes controversial, uses of RFID which include the 'chipping' of living beings. This has now become widespread for domestic pets, enabling them to be identified if lost and returned to their owners. It also facilitates their travelling between different countries, as the data on the chip includes details of vaccinations and other medical information, enabling their owners to take them on holiday more easily. (However, this is not always the outcome, as tags used for this purpose in the USA tend to be at a different frequency (125 kHz) from that specified by the International Standards Organisation (134.2 kHz) and as used in most of the rest of the world.)

For human beings, the external attachment of tags to criminals has become an alternative to prison in some instances, and has been generally accepted despite some concerns about its efficiency and effectiveness. However, there is less of a consensus about the use of RFID implants for human beings. While the benefits of health-related tagging are probably fairly widely accepted, the uses made by people such as Amal Grafstra of RFID implants in his hands to open the doors of his house and car, and to log on to his computer (www.amal.net/rfid.html) are perhaps more open to debate. Nevertheless, some nightclubs (Morton, 2004) have successfully persuaded some of their users that an RFID implant is an easy and convenient way to pay for their drinks.

Commercial uses

One of the few examples visible to the customer of large-scale adoption of RFID in the UK retail world is that of Marks & Spencer. The motivation for introducing RFID in this case was to improve stock control, and so improve sales. Aware of the importance of having all items available in the full range of sizes and colours all of the time, Marks & Spencer initially began tagging menswear to try to ensure that no customer seeking an outfit abandoned their purchase due to the unavailability of any one item.

Working on the basis that potential sales lost in this way – a jacket not bought because a matching pair of trousers could not be found in the right size; a suit not purchased because the shirt and tie required to go with it were not available – were a significant opportunity cost, the business case for RFID implementation became much more than a simple supply chain benefit and was soon extended to other categories of stock (Collins, 2004).

However, perhaps the largest RFID application in terms of scale and impact in the UK has been the introduction of Oyster cards by Transport for London, with millions of travellers now used to 'touching in and out', even if they may never have heard of RFID. The popularity of the system is a good example of way in which RFID can be applied to routine and often tedious tasks, in this case making an element of the commuting process much simpler and easier to use. This convenience no doubt explains much of the success and popularity of the scheme, although it should be noted that Transport for London has also used significant financial incentives to lead its customers along this path, and away from the more expensive, human interaction-based alternative of ticketing.

Disrupted libraries?

Probably the definitive disruptive technology in the library world since the early 1990s has been the internet, fundamentally changing traditional approaches to information management in many different ways. Indeed, from the point of view of many members of the public, it has been sufficiently disruptive for them to believe that it has done away with the need for libraries altogether.

So, is RFID also a disruptive technology for libraries? Applying Christensen's definition to the process of locating, borrowing and returning a book, it might be argued that the last major disruptive change in lending libraries was the move from closed to open access. This not only fundamentally changed the nature of the relationship between the reader, library staff and the library's contents, but also necessitated an entirely new technology to deliver the service in a completely different way.

For example, Cotgreve's indicator – the ingenious device developed to show whether an item was available for loan and where it could be found by library staff – suddenly became an irrelevance once library users were able to browse the shelves for themselves. Instead, new methods of library arrangement and navigational aids become necessary to exploit this change in approach, enabling and facilitating browsing and the serendipitous nature of libraries so highly valued by users today.

By extension, most developments in lending-library technology since the introduction of open access can be seen to have been only 'sustaining', providing (usually, but not always) better ways – Browne, photo-charging, barcodes – of recording transactions and devising procedures to provide various added-value services and/or save staff time.

RFID and libraries – a brief summary of the main applications

The disruptive quality offered to libraries by RFID is seen by its proponents to stem from its ability to change yet again the relationship between the customer, library staff and the book. Yet, while RFID's potential for revolutionizing stock management would seem likely to be its main selling point to library managers, its initial attraction has actually been a use to which it is not usually put elsewhere.

Self-service

Although the description of the RFID tag as a combined barcode/security device is not only simplistic and limiting in terms of realizing other potential applications, the customer-friendly self-service made possible by this combination of features is certainly at the heart of the attraction of RFID for most libraries. It also explains why libraries in particular have been so much quicker to adopt RFID than most retailers – the fast and convenient self-service it provides is a 'killer application' for libraries, where individual items are lent and returned possibly hundreds of times. Conversely, shopkeepers generally hope never to see an item again once it has left the premises. This alone means that the cost of the tag – the most expensive element in most systems – can be more easily justified by libraries, as the device will be used over and over again, as opposed to the single front-line transaction application in retail.

Security

The prevalence of RFID self-service installations obscures to some extent the level of use made by libraries of RFID as a security device, fulfilling the role otherwise undertaken by more traditional radio frequency (RF) or electromagnetic (EM) systems. Its use purely for this purpose, independent of self-service, is comparatively rare, mainly because self-service tends to be the main driver for installations, but also probably because there has been a certain amount of publicity suggesting that RFID is less effective in this area than RF or EM devices.

However, there is little firm evidence to support the supposition that RFID performs any less effectively than either RF or EM systems in minimizing loss by theft. One aspect – that it is usually easier to conceal an EM tag within the binding of a book, for example, so making it more difficult to disable – is certainly something that needs to be taken into account. Nevertheless, most library managers will also be aware that the value of such systems is essentially as a deterrent, rather than as a foolproof method of theft prevention. So, supporters of RFID point out that while RF and EM security systems have only limited other benefits to offer (essentially, their role in barcode-based self-service), RFID can also be used in a number of different ways.

Some libraries, however, do use these other security systems alongside RFID; this is particularly true of academic libraries, which often use EM security for non-book materials such as individual copies of journals, resulting in a hybrid approach which requires the introduction of dual-technology scanners to read both types of tag.

Stock control

The benefits that RFID offers the library manager in relation to stock control – particularly inventory and shelf-checking – are potentially equally as substantial as those provided to self-service and security. Perhaps surprisingly, however – especially considering that this is RFID's primary use elsewhere – adoption of these applications has been rather slower to catch on. This is partly due to difficulties in getting the hardware to perform satisfactorily, but perhaps also because the payback is rather less immediate.

In fact, there is a danger that RFID has already become synonymous with self-service for many library managers, to the extent that its potential for improving other library processes is overlooked. Later in this book, we shall explore other potential (and actual) applications of RFID in libraries which demonstrate its pervasive nature, resulting in additional benefits above and beyond that produced by self-service alone.

Summary

RFID has had a rapid impact on libraries, more so than on most other aspects of daily life. It operates at different frequencies, and its behaviour varies accordingly. RFID has been used in libraries mainly for self-service, but has the potential to revolutionize many aspects of library service delivery.

Chapter 2

RFID and libraries: the background and the basics

How did it all start? How does RFID work with existing library technology? Does it work with all stock?

The early days

As with many aspects of RFID, the location and timing of the earliest library experiments with RFID are a little unclear. Some commentators note that discussion of the potential of RFID for libraries dates back to the 1980s. There are also references to library books being RFID tagged as early as 1991 at University of Guelph library in Canada (RFID Gazette, 2006), although if so, it is unclear what use (if any) was made of the technology at the time – whatever it was, it seems not to have included self-service.

However – as is often the case with new inventions or their application in different fields – the two best-known early library projects began within a few months of each other in different parts of the world, with both having claimed to be 'the first RFID library in the world'.

Bukit Batok in Singapore went live in September 1998, and Rockefeller University in New York, USA, in February 1999. The differences between the two libraries are more than purely geographic, as the sectors and types of audience they serve are also fundamentally dissimilar. Bukit Batok is a community public library located in a shopping mall, with a stock of approximately 200,000 items and a membership of 28,000, while the Rockefeller University library in Manhattan, with a stock of around 500,000 items, serves mainly PhD students.

Despite differences in both audience and system supplier, and the pioneering nature of the applications, each library's use of RFID was nevertheless strikingly similar, exemplifying all of the features familiar to librarians looking to introduce the technology today – self-service, security, stock management and inventory control.

Both projects were also hailed as successes. For the Rockefeller University, system supplier Checkpoint (2000) claimed 'The Intelligent Library System™ has delivered on all of its promises, according to University Librarian Pat Mackey who attests that the system's technology has been exceedingly reliable.'

For Bukit Batok, the two main advantages were seen to be a reduction in waiting time for customers (from an average 90 minutes to 15 minutes (!)) and the ability to cope with ever-growing levels of business without the need to increase staffing levels. As a result, use of the technology had been extended to all the authority's 21 libraries by April 2002.

Despite these successes, further growth in library use of RFID worldwide was comparatively slow initially. Perhaps – when the cost of tags and the lack of any standard approach to the use of this technology in the library area are taken into account – it is surprising that anybody was prepared to take up a pioneering role in this area at all.

Three years on from these first installations, there were still fewer than 50 RFID libraries according to Richard W. Boss (2001), who contrasted this low take-up with the estimated 500,000 or more RFID installations in warehouses and retail outlets globally. Due to the high cost of tags, most of these library sites were small branches, although there were some major exceptions – both the University of Connecticut and the University of Nevada Las Vegas had over one million tagged items each.

However, less than four years later, Birgit Lindl of Bibliotheca (2005) estimated that there were over 300 RFID library sites, with around 120 million tagged items between them. This sudden and rapid growth in take-up saw the market respond with an increase in number of suppliers.

Checkpoint had provided the first system in the USA at Rockefeller University, while the system in Singapore had been developed jointly by Singapore Technologies Logitrack and the National Library Board. However, within six years, Laura Smart's summary of the marketplace for *Library Journal* (2004) was able to identify ten suppliers of 'integrated solutions' in the USA alone.

Declining costs

This supply-side growth, with its accompanying competition, had begun to help make RFID systems more affordable. In the same article, Smart detailed the estimates provided by individual suppliers to install an RFID system consisting of one self-issue unit, one self-return unit, one entrance gate and 200,000 tags. The lowest of these was $100,000–130,000, and the highest $175,000–275,000, with the average being around $150,000. As the cost of tags is usually the largest single element, it is clear that there had been a considerable fall in price since the first experiments six years before, when it had been in excess of $1 per tag.

The continuing rapid further fall in price of tags has been both a function of, and a factor in, the take-up of RFID in libraries since around 2004, to the point where one supplier in the UK alone had over 200 library sites in 2008, with the technology moving from being almost unheard of to comparatively mainstream in that time. The experience of one early adopter, the University of Central Lancashire (Mossop, 2008), shows precisely how stark this change in costs has been: 'We first began our exploration in the late 1990s, during the design stages for our Penrith campus . . . tags were £1 each . . . by the end of 2006 . . . the cost of tags had dropped from £1 to about 25p.' At the time of writing, depending on the quantity bought and the supplier, this figure had fallen to closer to 10p than to 20p.

RFID in libraries – how it works: the basics

Currently, at least, library RFID systems perform very few functions themselves and simply provide an alternative front end to the existing library management system (LMS). In the case of self-service, for example, this enables customers to interact with the LMS to carry out transactions themselves without the need for staff intervention – the RFID system simply relays the instructions it receives from the LMS onward to the customer, rather than initiating anything itself.

The link required between the RFID system and the LMS to enable this to happen is usually achieved by use of an interface protocol, which is discussed in more detail in Chapter 3.

The RFID tag, at a minimum, fulfils the function formerly performed by the barcode, providing the LMS with a unique identifier for each item and – if used for library cards as well – borrower. In fact, the RFID tag already has its own unique identifier provided by the manufacturer. However, as most libraries either will be running hybrid systems that still make some use of barcodes, or will be using RFID to replace a system currently using barcodes, the tag's original identifier is normally overwritten with the item's barcode number, to link it to the record for that item or borrower on the LMS database.

When the tag is brought within range of a scanner, the energy provided 'wakes' the tag and transmits its information to the scanner, which in turn communicates with the LMS, thus beginning the transaction.

Audiovisual material – a problem area . . .

This process assumes that the tag is able to communicate easily with the scanner, but unfortunately this is not always the case for most modern library services. As previously noted, while 13.56 MHz tags work perfectly well with the majority of library materials, they function less well with items containing metal. With most libraries having now moved forward (for most formats, at least) from analogue audiovisual products such as videotape and audiocassette (both of which work reasonably successfully with RFID) to Compact Discs (CDs) and Digital Versatile Discs (DVDs), it is unfortunate, to say the least, that RFID's performance with these newer formats is problematic.

At first sight, its performance also appears to be inconsistent in practice, with some libraries apparently achieving acceptable levels of tag readability and others failing significantly. However, this inconsistency appears to be attributable mainly to the construction of the disc, which is not uniform across all types. Although the basic principle of disc construction is common to all – two sides (one containing the material and the other a 'dummy' side or, in the case of double-sided discs, more material) made up of a sandwich of polycarbonate layers and a metal reflective layer and then glued together – the extent of the metal reflective layer is not. On some discs the metal extends into the 'hub' of the disc and so runs throughout the item, whereas on others the hub is plastic only.

On these latter discs it is possible to fit a 'doughnut' tag over the hub area, and it will generally work fairly successfully – although still less consistently than tags fitted to books, because of both its smaller size and its proximity to the metal in the rest of the disc. However, for discs in which the metal reflective layer runs across the hub, it will be virtually impossible to achieve any effective reading, as the tag will be located directly above the metal layer.

This clearly presents a major difficulty for libraries with audiovisual collections which wish to use RFID for self-service. A further complication is the fact that the proportion of discs with a full metal layer appears to be growing – accounting for 50% or more of some collections – and also that it is very difficult to judge from a simple visual inspection whether a disc is of one construction or the other.

The solution that some services, such as the London Borough of Sutton, have adopted is simply not to include audiovisual items in their self-service offer. Other approaches include use of a two-tag system – either placing a live tag on the disc's box and a dummy doughnut tag on the disc itself, or vice versa, depending on the disc's construction, thus enabling the tag to continue to be used for security purposes.

Some suppliers also offer 'booster' devices that can be fitted to a disc to amplify the signal sent from the tag; however, this may not always resolve the problem, as the resulting signal can still be very low and insufficient to be read across the usual metre or so between the tag and security scanner.

However, more importantly, there is concern in some quarters that placing tags of any kind on discs is increasingly likely to result in their not playing properly, or even possibly in some damage to the player. The likelihood of incorrect playing seems to be even greater with more modern discs, where flatness and uniformity appear to be essential for successful data transmission.

In addition to these concerns, there are also worries about the efficacy of the adhesives used to attach tags to discs. The ease with which some tags can be removed not only reduces their reliability as security devices, but also increases the likelihood of their becoming detached inside a player during use.

All of this has led some libraries to revert to using tagged 'safer' boxes, which use conventional magnetic locks to provide security while still enabling the benefits of RFID self-service - although they do add a further step to the process, requiring customers to unlock the safer box, having first checked the item out. Also, as this unlocking process will normally have to be carried out beyond any security gates, to ensure the integrity of the system, it results in a less than elegant solution which is entirely dependent on customers being aware that the safer has not been unlocked as part of the checkout process.

In summary, audiovisual collections are a significant potential problem area for RFID implementations in libraries, and one which needs to be considered in depth before going too far into the process.

Another complicated area – multipart items

One of the advantages that the RFID tag has in comparison to a barcode is its on-board memory, which can be used to great effect when dealing with complex, multipart sets. The most common approach to dealing with these is a 'parent–child' relationship between the tags used for each part: this is usually very successful, but there can be limits to the number of parts that can be dealt with in this way. One of the factors is that, despite the great speed at which the RFID scanner can read tags, some additional time may be required for the relationship between the items to be recognized. This in turn may mean that self-service customers may need to be advised to deal with these items in a way that is different from that for more usual materials.

Even worse, a combination of these two problems can occur with multipart audiovisual sets. If tags are attached to each disc, then even if only one disc in the set has metal running all through it, it can effectively mask the tags on the other discs and so prevent effective working.

Summary

These basic processes are common to all library RFID systems, while the problems are also present to different degrees and in different ways. However, the ways in which systems implement these processes and address these problems – and almost everything else – varies from supplier to supplier. There will also be some variation depending on the functions that RFID is being asked to provide. For example, libraries wanting to make use of RFID for what may be thought to be a comparatively straightforward purpose – security – will find that suppliers differ significantly in the way that they use the technology to achieve this. This aspect is explored more fully in Chapter 4, on standards and interoperability.

Chapter 3

RFID, library applications and the library management system

Wondering if you still need an LMS? If you do, how does RFID work with it? Is RFID just about self-service? What else can it do?

RFID and the LMS – why do you need both?

As we have seen, RFID - at least currently - is not a self-contained library product. It simply provides an alternative method of accessing an LMS, enabling library staff and customers to exploit the benefits of the technology - no need for line of sight, rapid read of multiple items - and so making the LMS more user friendly and able to carry out a wider range of tasks.

Some library managers have queried why, if this is the case, RFID has to be developed in a specific way for application in libraries if it simply provides what is a 'front end' to an existing technology - and some of them, to a greater or lesser degree, have been successful; for example, through the use of generic terminals for self-service.

Others have questioned the split between RFID and LMS, and wondered why suppliers do not simply integrate the technologies into one product - an RFID-enabled LMS. There are certainly examples of companies that provide both technologies - VTLS in the USA, and DS in the UK being two companies that supply both LMS and RFID systems, although their provision of one does not preclude supply of the other by another company. Similarly, some LMS suppliers have formed strategic partnerships with RFID suppliers, and vice versa, but have understandably not limited themselves to those liaisons, as their existing customers may well wish to choose a system that falls outside such arrangements.

Either way, it is very likely at present that most libraries will have to deal with two different companies (at least) when installing an RFID system. The reason for this perhaps relates rather more to the current commercial state of the library technology market than to the technology itself. It would be possible to develop a fully integrated RFID-enabled LMS, but it appears to require a level of investment and development which neither LMS nor RFID suppliers currently wish, or are able, to contemplate.

The changing market for LMS

This is not surprising in light of the debate regarding the future of the LMS that has been under way since the late 1990s. The concept of a fully integrated LMS - something of a 'holy grail' for library managers during the 1980s and early 1990s - has become less and less popular in the early 21st century. This is partly because some libraries have reviewed their requirements in light of changing technology and observed the development of individual packages able to fulfil most of the functions of the LMS - acquisitions, database management and so on - which come from outside the library world and which use more generic (and therefore cheaper) solutions. Meanwhile, the development of open source LMS in the USA and elsewhere (www.oss4Lib.org and www.koha.org for example) has attracted many library managers disillusioned by the apparent inability of commercial LMS suppliers to respond to wish-list requirements within a timeframe of less than five years.

This perceived inflexibility can be seen as a function of the level of consolidation in the LMS market. The rapid merging of LMS companies since the late 1990s has resulted in greatly reduced choice for the consumer. Some commentators attribute this to the entry of venture capitalists into the market, while there has also been an element of larger companies buying out smaller ones. Either way, the increasing need to improve efficiency and financial performance that has accompanied these moves has also seen most suppliers having to reduce programmer and development capacity.

Conversely, most RFID suppliers – at least initially – knew little about the library market, and probably came into it attracted by its potential to expand the take-up of RFID at the item-tagging level, and so to sell more tags. The fact that they were also able to adapt their existing products to this new scenario with comparatively little input understandably made libraries a very attractive diversification prospect for RFID providers and aggregators, while the existence of an established system – the LMS – to manage the underlying transactions will no doubt have made the prospect even more attractive.

RFID suppliers were fortunate not only to have such an existing system to link to, obviating the need to worry about designing something from the ground up to do all the hard work involved in library transactions, but also for there to be a ready-made interface that enabled their product and the LMS to speak to each other. The interface used by virtually all systems for this purpose is the Standard Interchange Protocol (SIP) produced by 3M. The latest version, first published in 1997 but updated frequently since (3M Library Systems, 2006), includes extra messages and new fields for existing messages, and is called SIP2: for the sake of simplicity, however, the protocol is referred to as SIP throughout this book.

SIP

SIP was originally developed by 3M as an interface protocol to enable its own barcode-based self-service products to work with any LMS, but it has subsequently become the means by which many other third-party products – manufactured by a great variety of companies – interoperate with an LMS. These range from self-payment packages to e-books, and 3M has been happy to allow SIP to be used by libraries around the world to expand their services in this way. LMS suppliers are also understandably keen to use a ready-made solution which adds value to their product – although customers will want to know how much their suppliers are going to charge them for the privilege of using it.

SIP or NCIP?

However, although SIP is frequently referred to as a de facto standard, it should be remembered that it is more accurately a protocol, and that its origin as a proprietary 3M solution means that it is neither managed by an independent standards authority nor subject to the usual requirements that standards are expected to fulfil. It is also worth noting that, as different LMS and RFID suppliers adapt and add to SIP to improve the way that their systems function, it is not therefore directly interoperable – or interchangeable – between individual LMS. The outcome is that SIP, depending on the LMS being used, is actually a range of proprietary applications of a proprietary protocol. As a result, if a library changes its LMS but retains its RFID existing system, it is highly likely that the SIP arrangements will have to be changed as well.

A solution to this appeared to be imminent in 2002 with the introduction in the USA of NCIP, the National Information Standards Organisation's Circulation Interchange Protocol, or, more formally, ANSI/NISO Z39.83-200x. This ambitious standard's aim was threefold, seeking to enable and standardize interoperability between individual LMS for:

■   interlibrary loans
■   consortial borrowing
■   self-service.

The self-service element of NCIP recognized the pre-eminence of SIP in this area, and essentially used much of SIP's content , thus developing an actual standard from a de facto one.

Unfortunately, NCIP's ambitious objective in trying to cover so much ground resulted in a very low adoption rate, with the result that it has had to be fundamentally rethought. Indeed, the lack of acceptance of NCIP has been seen by some to indicate the end of the kind of generic, broad-based approach to producing standards that NCIP exemplifies, with much more specific, smaller-scale, bottom-up rather than top-down projects now more likely to become the norm.

At the time of writing, NCIP is still being reviewed and so SIP remains the most common means of providing an interface between RFID and the

LMS, and looks set to continue so for some time. Whether NCIP finally prevails or not, it may be that technology will overtake it, with some new approach – possibly based on web services – replacing it in due course.

In the mean time, libraries looking to adopt RFID will need to be aware that systems may claim to be 'sIP compliant', but that this statement may cover a range of levels of compliance and does not necessarily guarantee that their particular LMS will be able to speak to a specific RFID system at all, or (more likely) that all of the functions they require will be operational.

Back-up: is offline service the same as online?

Many new adopters, having been impressed with the features that RFID has to offer, have investigated another aspect of the RFID/LMS relationship. Understandably they want to ensure that its benefits – self-service in particular – are available for the maximum amount of time. Consequently, they query why – even if the LMS and RFID systems cannot be merged into one – self-service should not function fully when there is a problem with the LMS and the system has to go into back-up. This is increasingly demanded by academic libraries in particular, who want to be able to guarantee 24-hour access to their collections; in such cases, even when there are no problems with the LMS, the requirement for a certain amount of downtime to carry out back-up and 'overnight' processes will result in a similar situation.

Self-service will, of course, continue to be available in most cases, but without the level of sophistication provided by the LMS – there will be no facility to recognize different borrower types and privileges, or varied loan periods, for example. One solution to this is seen to be the provision of more data on the item tag, enabling the system to recognize material types without the need for recourse to the LMS database. However, this would then also require the RFID system to be aware of the library's borrowing rules for each type of material and, by extension, of the privileges of each category of borrower, and to have a method of combining the two in a meaningful way. In short, the RFID system would need to fulfil all the functions of the LMS.

This illustrates the crux of the question about the relationship between the RFID system and the LMS, and how they are currently interdependent. At present, while some LMS suppliers offer an 'integrated' approach to RFID, there currently seems to be little likelihood of an RFID supplier offering a system that would work completely independently of an LMS.

Self-payment

A further complication arises where self-payment is incorporated into self-service. This is already a process that can be implemented using a wide variety of formats and types of payment device, which can include:

- simple coin-operated mechanisms which are unable to give change
- orthodox debit and credit cards, with or without 'chip and pin' technology
- 'smart' library cards that contain an electronic purse.

More recently – and more usefully for libraries, considering the very low value of most of their transactions – contactless RFID cards such as Barclaycard's 'OnePulse' and Mastercard's 'Paypass' have become available. The advantage of these cards (apart from the fact that they are usually multifunctional, acting as credit cards as well as fulfilling the other roles, such as functioning as an Oyster card in London) is that they are specifically designed to deal with transactions below £10. This technology, designed to help do away with the need to carry small change, is also being made available within mobile phones and electronic watches.

However, despite this great array of means for receiving payments from customers, the library is usually still entirely dependent on the LMS to determine whether or not the customer owes any money in the first place and, if so, how much. If the LMS has to go into back-up, then some alternative means of providing this information has to be found. Again, this would require the RFID system somehow to be aware of the current state of the customer's transactions.

Staff processes

At first sight it would seem that, where staff are involved in issuing and discharging material through LMS terminals, they should also be able to benefit from the advantages arising from RFID. It is certainly true that processes performed by staff at the counter can often be streamlined to some extent via to RFID – and many who use the RFID system's screens as a front end to the LMS have said that they would not wish to have to revert to the old way of working – but there have been some limits to this.

The main limit has been that the speedy reading of multiple items – one of the most useful features of RFID self-service – has not been possible on staff stations. The reason for this is that it is enabled by SIP, which is not available on the staff side. However, some suppliers now offer software which enables staff-operated units to simulate bulk reading of multiple items. In addition to making issuing and discharging material much easier, this also makes an important contribution to the use of RFID in speeding up the acquisitions process.

Self-service and the LMS – some other complications
Blocks

Unfortunately, because the self-service unit simply receives instructions from the LMS via SIP, there are a number of things it is unable to do as a result.

Perhaps the most limiting of these is that – unlike a member of staff – it is generally unable to differentiate between the levels of importance of the messages it receives from the LMS. Consequently, the many non-critical blocks that an LMS might place on a transaction, and which staff may routinely override, result in the customer being unable to complete the process and being asked to seek staff help. The number and frequency of this type of problem will vary according to the LMS, but invariably, the more sophisticated the system, the more blocks there will be.

Some of these blocks may be the result of very simple situations, and may occur in each of the usual modes of operation – issue, discharge and renew. Obvious examples are where items have not been tagged, or where tags have been programmed incorrectly or not at all, but more frequently they result from exception reports being sent to the self-service unit by the LMS, relating to either the item or the customer. Examples include:

- Item has been reserved by a different borrower
- Item is still recorded as on loan to a different borrower
- Item belongs to a different library
- Item is for use in the library only
- Borrower has exceeded lending limit
- Borrower has outstanding charges
- Borrower's membership has elapsed.

In each of these cases, a member of staff should be able to resolve these situations (and any combination of them) quickly and easily, but it is unlikely that the LMS and RFID system will be able to be programmed to deal with them routinely – and probably undesirable as well: if the exceptions were unimportant, why put them into the LMS in the first place?

Absence of blocks

Generally speaking, the problems caused by blocks will be more of an irritant than a show stopper. However, there are some situations where the absence of human intervention can be much more problematic and can arise not from blocks, but from their absence. The most important category of this type is where there are legal limitations on what individual customers may borrow. A specific example of this from the UK is the age restriction on the purchase and loan of DVDs/videos as defined by the 1984 Video Recordings Act.

This Act makes it an offence to lend an age-restricted film to anybody too young to borrow it. Most library services will have their LMS set up to deal with this, by ensuring that the parameters prevent the issue of certain material types – such as '18' classified DVDs – to borrowers below that age. In normal circumstances, this is further reinforced by staff, who can intervene if it is clear that a young person has borrowed the ticket of an older customer in an attempt to obtain such an item.

The advice from some Trading Standards officers, however, is that, as self-service does not provide this additional level of security, NO age-restricted material should be lent in this way. For any library hoping to achieve high levels of self-issue, this is clearly very limiting: all loans of DVDs would thus have to be dealt with by staff so as to ensure that no illegal activity occured. It should be said that such advice is not universal, but the possibility that a library service may have no serious defence if challenged in this area will naturally be something that it will want to consider in some depth.

The crux of this problem appears to be that a library card usually has no built-in security to prevent its use by a person other than the one to whom it is registered. As a result, one of the few general defences to the Act – that 'the accused took all reasonable precautions and exercised all due diligence to avoid the commission of the offence by any person under his control' – becomes unavailable. Consequently, if there is nothing to prevent a library card being misused in this way, then it would appear that this Trading Standards advice would have to be followed.

However, many LMS provide a PIN (Personal Identification Number) facility to prevent this kind of unauthorized use, which is incorporated into the self-service process. It is not currently clear whether use of this facility would satisfy a legal challenge or not, but many library services rely on this, arguing that it does demonstrate that they have done all they can to prevent unauthorized borrowing, and that it is at least as effective as any intervention provided by staff.

There are further, more specific questions, that will need to be asked regarding the relationship between the RFID system and the LMS, and these are detailed in Chapter 10.

RFID and stock control
Hand-held devices

Although self-service has been the main focus for most RFID installations in libraries – and has certainly provided the quickest and most easily determinable return on investment – it is quite possible that the possibilities that RFID opens up for improvements in stock management may be of greater long-term benefit to library managers.

In fact, as we have seen, most non-library RFID applications have been related in some way to stock control and logistics, and so this would seem to be an area where libraries should be able to achieve a further return on investment in addition to that provided by self-service.

To date, most of this has been achieved through the use of hand-held devices, the best known example of which is probably 3M's Digital Library Assistant. They have demonstrated that stock inventory checking can now be realistically completed on a regular basis in a matter of hours, rather than weeks or months, as had previously been the case for most libraries. Indeed, the Vatican Library has adopted RFID for precisely this reason, rather than for self-service (for which it has little need) (Young, 2004).

In addition, by downloading reports created by the LMS, it is possible to use these devices to 'search and find' items that have been identified for circulation to another library as requests, or indeed any 'exception' status created as part of automatic stock editing processes, again reducing the amount of time required for these routine elements of library work. Items that have been misplaced can also be located and reshelved in the correct sequence.

However, there have been concerns about the efficiency of hand-held devices in specific situations, with problems being encountered as a result of the co-location of large numbers of thin books, for example, making it difficult for the device's scanner to differentiate between tags. Other limitations can be caused by metal shelves or bookends masking the presence of tags, the presence of CD-ROMs in books, and the use of metallic foil on book covers. The difficulties referred to in Chapter 2 relating to audiovisual material may obviously arise in this context too, meaning that the use of hand-held devices to manage CDs or DVDs is likely to be very problematic.

There are also basic differences in the way different RFID systems use the tag for these purposes, as with self-service. Some systems rely on downloading files to the LMS to obtain full details for each item, while others use additional information loaded on the tag for this purpose. Questions then arise, as previously noted, about the location of the definitive information about each item, and the need to keep it updated. If there is a discrepancy, for any reason, between the data on the tag and that in the LMS catalogue, which is deemed to be the correct data? This, in turn, raises a question that is at once both philosophical and pragmatic: does the true catalogue rest in the LMS database, or in the tags in the books on the shelf?

As a result of these and similar questions, it has taken rather longer than they had hoped for stock management benefits to be realized by most libraries. However, the performance of hand-held scanners continues to improve, and their use to grow. This is being helped by the development of more sophisticated software packages for stock management, whether as an integrated part of an LMS, or as an additional, externally produced module such as Bridgeall's SmartSM, which has been further developed to integrate with RFID processes.

Smart shelves

Smart shelves have been seen as a potentially more elegant and effective solution to stock management questions. The addition of scanners to individual shelves, recording item activity on a continuous basis, is able to give a much more detailed picture of stock use than that provided by the occasional use of hand-held devices.

The downside of smart shelves, however, is their cost and reliability. Although there have been pilot projects – perhaps the best-known example being the Metro Group Future Store in Rheinberg, Germany (www.future-store.org) – their success has been comparatively limited. Initially, this was partly to do with the technology's requirement for bulky coaxial cable connections and consequent lack of flexibility; later generations have been less cumbersome, making use of different kinds of antennae, but they remain expensive and the level of investment required by a library remains too high for this solution to be a realistic option for most – at least for the time being.

However, other approaches to the same concept, such as Intellident's SmartBlade device (www.intellident.co.uk/4.00/en/downloads/SMDA1018. pdf), which allows existing shelving to be retrofitted with scanners, suggest that it may be possible for such a feature to become more affordable for libraries in the near future. If so, then the potential that RFID clearly has to improve library stock management processes comes much closer to being achievable. It also offers the opportunity to learn much more about in-library use of material, most of which is currently unknowable. For example, although reference material is increasingly provided electronically in most libraries, the long-standing question of how to measure the in-library use of material, including reference books, could be resolved by such an application.

Acquisitions
Procedures and technology

The application of scanners to the acquisitions process also offers the potential to reduce the confusingly large number of transactions involved in getting the book from the publisher to the library shelf. Nevertheless, there are again a number of areas of work that will need to be addressed for this to succeed.

Much of this, unsurprisingly, will relate to the way that the LMS acquisitions module works. The use of RFID in conjunction with the order fulfilment module of EDI (Electronic Data Interchange) should make it possible to make the processes of receipting and adding copy details to bibliographic records much more efficient, but the detail of these processes will need to be reviewed before they work in an optimum way. The eventual outcome should be that simply scanning a box of books, rather than having to deal with each copy individually, is all that is needed to complete the process. However, this will also be dependent on staff LMS units being able to deal with bulk multiple tag readings, as mentioned earlier.

However, there is a much broader question to resolve, before all of this becomes reality, regarding the effectiveness of 13.56 MHz tags in this type of activity. Although well suited to the requirements of self-service, High Frequency tags have not always been seen as completely effective at item level in the supply chain environment, where 100% read rate of multiple tags in a consignment is essential. It was primarily for this reason that the only RFID applications to date in the book trade – Selexys in the Netherlands and Byblos Amoreiras in Lisbon – adopted the UHF approach, as experiments with HF tags failed to demonstrate the required level of reliability when attempting to read box-loads of material.

Nevertheless, the continuing development of tag and scanner performance may mean that HF tags will be able to perform this function sufficiently consistently to enable them to be used confidently in this area before too long; the introduction of ISO/IEC 18000-3 Mode 3 tags in particular (see Chapter 4) offers some hope of this. This kind of development means, equally, that there is no certainty at this stage that UHF will be the ultimate choice of the book trade.

Questions of frequency and technology to one side, however, the application of RFID to the library acquisitions process is still not entirely straightforward. In fact, the initial effect of introducing RFID into the library supply chain is simply to add something else that needs to be done to the book – the application of the tag.

Book processing and servicing

If a library service has a mix of RFID and non-RFID libraries, then RFID will unfortunately mean simply the addition of yet another process to which books are subjected as part of being made 'shelf ready' – the application and programming of a tag in addition to the stationery, jacketing and labelling (or 'licking and sticking', as library suppliers often call it). While all these elements contribute to the speed and efficiency of issuing, discharging and shelving a book on a day-to-day basis later on in its life, they nevertheless make its initial progress to the shelf very tortuous.

Not only that, but some RFID suppliers have stipulated that RFID tags should be placed in specific, and different, places by the book supplier – for example, the tag in book one should go on the inside back cover, top right corner; in book two, lower left corner, and so on. The intention behind this is to make it easier for hand-held scanners find books when undertaking stock management procedures, as placing tags in the same place in each book, and so reducing the space between them, may affect the effectiveness of these devices.

However, in practice, the effectiveness of this approach is limited by the way in which book suppliers tend to work – processing the same title for different libraries at the same time, rather than different books for the same library sequentially. As a result, the additional time spent by book suppliers in this way is unlikely to mean that books will be shelved in any one library with tag positions distributed in this manner – it is likely to be just as effective, if not more so, and easier for the book supplier if different tag locations are used on different titles rather than on different copies of the same title.

The main benefit of RFID, however, in a system where all libraries are RFID-enabled, is that – at least in theory – there is plenty of scope for reducing the level of processing done to books:

- Universal self-service and provision of receipts means date labels are no longer necessary.
- RFID identification means that barcodes are no longer required.
- RFID security obviates the need for a separate tag.

There are some arguments for retaining some of these elements – barcodes provide an easy visual check of the book's identifier and can be overprinted onto the tag if necessary; some customers prefer to have a date label rather than a receipt. However, the potential cost savings and improvements in speed of supply resulting from such simplification are likely to provide a substantial incentive not to keep them.

Navigating the library

The use of RFID, possibly in conjunction with other technologies, to enable customers to find their way around the library or to locate a specific item, is something which has been mooted for some time. Some examples of this have begun to appear since around 2005.

Kevin Curran and Martin Porter (2007) describe how RFID's ability to act as a 'location determination technology' can be exploited to speed up the way in which a customer can find a book. A prototype, using a combination of a Personal Digital Assistant (PDA) (to host the applications) incorporating a scanner, and a wireless network, enables the user to scan across shelves until the desired book is identified by the PDA, even if the book is misplaced. While there are clearly echoes here of most RFID suppliers' hand-held devices, the relatively low cost of a PDA-type solution makes the possibility of a unit for the customer, rather than staff, much more likely.

An application of this type which is both more specific and more fully realized can be found as part of the Bibliotek 2007 project in Umea,

Sweden, which, among other things, is designed to produce 'the world's most accessible library' (Umea, 2007). One element of the project is 'audioindex', which was developed to help visually impaired people (VIPs) browse the library's collection of audiobooks as easily as sighted people. Through use of a hand-held scanner and a headset, VIPs are able to find their way around the library to the audiobook collection, and then interrogate RFID tags attached to individual audiobooks to receive an audio description of the item's author and title and a summary of its content.

Summary

RFID currently acts as the 'front end' for the LMS: the advantage of this is that the move to RFID (and RFID self-service in particular) is comparatively straightforward, requiring only an interface (currently provided by SIP) to make it work. The disadvantage is that this requires two systems to work together – which is not always easy to achieve – and it also limits the potential that RFID offers to transform other aspects of library work.

This may change as the LMS market reflects changes in demand, or possibly as forms of interface between the LMS and RFID are developed.

Chapter 4

Standards and interoperability

Need to know about standards? Are there any? Who produces them? What effect do they have?

Standards, or free for all?

One of the principal contributory factors to the rapid take-up of RFID systems in the library world has been the view – taken by vendors and buyers alike – that solutions for individual libraries or networks can be considered to be closed loops. In such a scenario, there is no need to be concerned about standards or interoperability with other libraries – let alone other organizations – as the emphasis is entirely on RFID's performance within the local context.

This is perhaps not too surprising. It is arguable that – despite a raft of standards relating to cataloguing, indexing and other professional staples – it is only comparatively recently (since the coming of the internet?) that interoperability has been the focus of much attention in the world of library technology, with most systems being largely proprietary.

More specifically – and crucially – the level of interoperability between different manufacturers' LMS has been very low. Even though this has begun to change, it still remains a major concern and has long been an obstacle to joint working. One example of this (among many) is a project begun in 1999/2000, jointly funded by the UK's Department of Culture Media and Sport and the Wolfson Foundation (DCMS, 2000), which saw the creation of a public library cooperative organization in the east of England, called CO-EAST, whose primary remit included the provision of unmediated interlibrary loans between the 14 authorities in the region, allowing the customers of one library service to place holds on material held by any of the others.

For this to work, it was necessary to get three different LMS to communicate with each other, providing not only the facility to search individual catalogues – a comparatively straightforward project – but also to recognize the details and status of the members of 14 different library services. Unfortunately, this simple-sounding concept proved impossible to put into practice, and some six years after CO-EAST was set up (and despite many other achievements) it was disbanded, with its initial objective still unfulfilled.

Eventually, standards that were nascent at the time might have been able to provide a solution to this problem, but at the time it proved impossible to achieve CO-EAST's original aim, at least with the resources available to it. It is probably less surprising, then, that a much newer technology such as RFID should also exhibit problems of compatibility between different suppliers' systems.

Interoperability – is it really needed?

Conversely, one benefit of this lack of standards has been that a variety of library RFID systems has now been developed, each of which uses the technology in different ways, with different strengths and weaknesses, and from which librarians can select according to their own particular requirements. Some library managers might also query the emphasis on interoperability: if interlibrary loans, for example, account for only 1–2% of a library service's transactions, why should it be concerned about being able to read tags from other systems?

It should also be noted that interoperability of tags in itself is not the solution to this problem – at least, not unless their data content goes beyond a simple unique identifier – as can be seen by looking at the current position with barcodes. Although there are standards relating to barcodes which make them readable by different systems, this is of no advantage whatsoever if the information they contain – essentially an accession number – is not linked to anything meaningful in the receiving library's database. Although most LMS enable the creation of records 'on the fly' for items that they do not recognize, enabling the barcode to be used if desired, this is not really interoperability in any real sense of the term.

Where library services act in consortia in their use of LMS, this sharing of systems does enable seamless interlibrary loans between them. However, it is the use of an LMS in common and a shared database that makes this possible, rather than the use of standard barcodes (although they are clearly essential as well).

It's not just about interoperability . . .

The disadvantages resulting from a lack of standards are significant, however, and are not limited simply to the fact that different systems will not be able to communicate with each other. (There is also an argument that there might be a much higher level of interlending – and library use generally – if a wider public were made aware of all the holdings of libraries elsewhere.)

A less immediate but certainly more financially crucial outcome is fragmentation of the market, where the tag used by each system may be slightly different, thus denying any economies of scale for suppliers. Consequently, prices will remain higher than they would if there were a generic tag used by all libraries.

Another longer-term consideration is that a library service needs to be confident not only that tag supply is going to be sustainable in the future, but also that it will not be faced with the need to retag its material if looking to replace its RFID system at a later date – a problem already faced by some early adopters.

So, just how different can tags be? In fact, the differences between systems in the way they have used tags since the late 1990s have been very wide ranging, in terms of both size of memory and the functions they perform. For example, the Tagsys tag was originally 74 bit with an integrated security element. In contrast, Checkpoint's original standard library tag was 95 bit, but used the LMS to provide the security information. 3M's tag was originally 256 bit, Intellident's 512 bit, while Bibliotheca's is 1024 bit.

The only feature common to all of the original systems was that they used the 13.56 MHz frequency – but, as has been noted, even this is now changing, as Australian company Civica has begun to install UHF (920 MHz) RFID systems in libraries, the first of these being in Blacktown (Blacktown City Council, 2008).

What standards are there?

All of this may give the impression that the world of RFID is standard free, but, not surprisingly – as RFID is used in thousands of non-library situations on a day-to-day basis and has been for some time – there are many standards that control the ways in which RFID should work.

Not only are there many standards, but there are also many different bodies producing them. This is a very complex area, and its detailed examination is somewhat outside the scope of this book. However, in summary, the main bodies include the International Standards Organisation (ISO); the International Electrotechnical Commission (IEC); the ITU-T (the Telecommunication Standardization Sector of the United Nations agency for information and communication technologies); the European Telecommunications Standards Institute (ETSI); and EPCGlobal.

EPCGlobal is of particular interest in relation to RFID, due to its link to the concept of the 'internet of things', originally developed by the Auto-ID centre at the Massachusetts Institute of Technology to produce 'an open architecture for creating a seamless global network of physical objects', using the object naming service (ONS) managed by VeriSign. This was further developed into the Electronic Product Code Global Network by EPCGlobal, following the closure of the Auto-ID Centre in 2003. Within this worldwide network, a unique identifier on each RFID tag, registered on the ONS, enables the tag to be traced by anybody with access to the system.

Not surprisingly, these different bodies have tended to work at different speeds and in different ways, resulting in a great deal of concern about lack of coordination and possible duplication – or divergence – in effort and outcome. This has recently begun to be addressed by the Global RFID

Interoperability Forum for Standards (2008), although there is still some considerable way to go before this is resolved to any substantial degree.

However, despite this multiplicity of organizations, there are comparatively few international standards that relate to the areas of RFID currently used by libraries. In fact, at the time of writing, there is only one international standard that relates to any part of RFID used in libraries, which is ISO/IEC 18000. The first part of this, which is, strictly speaking, a series of separate but related standards rather than one discrete one, is ISO/IEC 18000-1. This provides definitions of parameters that need to be determined in any standardized air interface definition (that is, the way that tags and scanners communicate with each other) for tags covered by the standard. Subsequent parts relate to tags at specific frequencies, and so ISO/IEC 18000-3 is the one of interest to most libraries, as it covers 13.56MHz tags. However, it should be noted that this standard is not library specific: it simply defines some elements of the way in which the tags used by most libraries should behave.

Sometimes, instead of ISO/IEC 18000, suppliers refer (confusingly) to ISO/IEC 15693, although in fact that standard relates to smart cards, rather than to tags. This is because, for a short time, the same standard was used for both tags and cards, as the technology involved was essentially the same; however, separate standards were then created for each, to enable them to be developed independently. ISO/IEC 15693 will, of course, still be of interest to libraries planning to introduce smart library cards.

The key aspect of ISO/IEC 18000 from a library point of view is that it regulates only the way in which tags and scanners should communicate with each other – the 'air interface'. As 13.56 MHz tags are used in a huge range of different settings and environments, the standard does not address anything that is library specific, such as mandating how data should be formatted on a tag, or even which data should be included. It is essentially a standard that defines how the technology should work, rather than any particular application of it.

This, in part, explains the variety of ways in which suppliers have been able to use otherwise apparently similar tags – in the absence of any standardization of content or format, they have been free to customise the tag in the ways that best suit their system.

As with memory size and other tag elements, the way that suppliers have viewed the data that needs to be held on a tag has also differed considerably. Indeed, there is an almost philosophical difference in approach to the amount of data that is included on a tag.

Licence plate or full data?

At one extreme, libraries can simply encode the tag with a unique identifier: this 'licence-plate' method relies on the LMS for all detailed information about the item to which the tag is attached. Conversely, some suppliers offer inclusion of a much greater range of data, such as the bulk of the item's bibliographic record, details of the owning library and much more. Still other suppliers, taking the view that the customer is always right, offer both options, leading to a situation where users of the same system can have their tags encoded with different levels of data, and in different ways.

Each of these approaches has its benefits and disadvantages: the 'licence plate' has the advantage of simplicity, and also means that any updating of information about the item is done only once – on the library management system. It also conforms to the standard IT principle that – as far as possible – data should be held in one place only, and so avoids the danger of different versions of the same information being held in the system.

However, one reason originally provided by some RFID suppliers for using this approach – that tags can be read more quickly if they hold less data, and so provide faster self-service – is not correct. Scanners can be tuned to read specific parts of a tag and not others in particular circumstances, and so can be set at self-service points to read only the unique identifier if that is all that is required. Other data can still be held elsewhere on the tag, with no effect on the speed of operation.

On the other hand, RFID tags are increasingly capable of holding a significant amount of information, much of which may be of use in specific library settings – during the acquisitions process; when carrying out stock taking or shelf tidying; when the item is on interlibrary loan; or when the LMS is in back-up. In addition – as tags have a rewrite facility, enabling them to be reprogrammed for different purposes at different stages in the life cycle of the item to which they are attached - supporters of this approach contend that this makes much better use of the RFID tag's adaptability and capacity, rather than simply duplicating the barcode number.

These differences in approach apply not only to system suppliers, but also to countries. In the absence of any international tag data standards, a number of countries have developed their own national standards - including the Netherlands, Denmark, Finland and France. As a very broad generalization, these national standards have favoured both a significant amount of data on the tag, and a standard positioning of specific elements of that data within the tag's structure. They have not, however, resulted in any agreement on which items should be mandatory, nor where they should be located on the tag. As a result, each of these national standards is unique, with its own rules, despite a similar aim of making the most use of the tag's capacity and versatility.

This very specific and mandatory use of data on the tag is essentially a reflection of the structures of the library supply chain and interlibrary loan systems in these countries, which tend to be centralized and where the responsibility for, and purpose of, each element in the movement of a book from publisher to library shelf is clearly defined.

In such a situation, the RFID tag and its memory capacity can be exploited very effectively and used to their fullest extent to benefit all parties involved. As a result, information about media type, supplier, order number, invoice number and supply stage are not only useful but essential if the tag is to fulfil all that is asked of it in the supply chain. Similarly, use of the International Standard Identifier for Libraries (ISIL) to identify the owning and borrowing library for interlibrary loan transactions enables the tag to greatly simplify all the processes involved in supplying requested material between different library authorities.

At the other extreme, the UK, the USA and Australia - where such centralized approaches are much less in evidence - have tended to want rather less data on the tag, and certainly less that is compulsory. Regardless of the amount of data, however, they have also tended to support a more flexible approach to the way the data is encoded.

ISO 28560 – towards a standard library data model

It is not surprising, therefore, that the ISO Working Group tasked with producing a standard data model for library RFID tags – ISC/TC46/SC4 (see www.bs.dk/standards/rfid/, or for 2008 onwards http://biblstandard. dk/rfid) – has found it impossible to reconcile these positions. Instead, it has proposed a standard – ISO 28560 – comprising three parts and, subject to final confirmation, due to be published in 2009. It specifically builds on the work done in ISO/IEC 18000 by adopting the tag memory architecture outlined in ISO/IEC 18000-3 for Mode 1 tags, and so supports the ever-increasing number of libraries using technology based on that standard.

As a result, ISO 28560 is not able to accommodate such possible future developments as a major move by libraries to UHF, for example, as tags at those frequencies have a different memory architecture, defined by ISO/IEC 18000-6. Instead, it proposes that a watching brief should be kept on future developments, asserting that it is currently impossible to predict how the industry might change in future. In particular, it says that a wholesale move by libraries to UHF is far from certain, and suggests that the more significant advances in technology may well occur in the HF area, particularly in light of the imminent introduction of ISO/IEC 18000-3 Mode 3 tags: these will be interoperable with Mode 1 tags, but will offer improved functionality and performance.

In terms of the structure of the standard, Part 1 relates to general requirements and defines the data fields, such as unique identifier, ownership, MARC/ONIX data and so on that may be used when encoding tags for libraries. However, Parts 2 and 3 are mutually exclusive.

Part 2 specifies a model using the flexible approach preferred mainly by the UK, USA and Australia. It uses two existing standards – ISO/IEC 15961 and 15962 – to provide a tag data protocol, specifying how data should be exchanged between the LMS and the RFID reader, and providing encoding rules for the data to be placed on the tag, as well as logical memory functions. It uses object identifiers to represent data elements, which in turn conserves tag space.

Part 3 specifies how to adopt the approach preferred mainly by northern European countries, using fixed-length encoding. As implied by this description, this approach specifies a very prescriptive approach to which data elements should be stored where, although the use of national profiles for some elements is allowed, so long as they still conform to the content parameters of the overall standard.

Despite these differences in approach, both Parts 2 and 3 make only the unique identifier – or Primary Item Identifier, as it is referred to – a mandatory field, with all other elements optional. However, it also specifies that, for this identifier to be truly unique, it needs to incorporate additional identifiers for the owning library (usually the ISIL) and the application for which it is being programmed (see Application Family Identifier below).

The standard also provides advice about other more general questions, such as the locking (or otherwise) of data elements, and is not restricted entirely to matters relating to the tag alone. It also specifies that library RFID readers should be based on the open architecture standards defined by ISO/IEC's JTC1 SC31 WG4, 'RFID for Item Management', so enabling interoperability between any combination of tags and readers provided by different manufacturers.

However, just as importantly, the standard also provides detailed information on how libraries can migrate from their existing arrangements to conform to these new requirements. This advice on migration is essential, as, perhaps surprisingly, it is highly unlikely that any existing library RFID systems currently conform precisely to this standard, whether using the flexible or fixed method.

For example, although the Part 3 specification enables the fixed kind of approach preferred by countries such as Denmark and the Netherlands, it is nevertheless different from each of the national standards for those countries (as they, in turn, are different from each other).

Meanwhile, most libraries in the UK, Australia, USA and other countries with more decentralized library arrangements, which tend to have only a simple accession/barcode number on the tag, will still need to amend the information on their tags to conform to Part 2. They are unlikely currently to fulfil the requirement for a globally unique identifier, using the ISIL and AFI, and it is also probable that they do not use the recommended tag data protocol.

As a result, the major tasks facing bodies interested in promoting the use of standards in library RFID in the near future will be not only to facilitate a common approach to the adoption of this standard, but also to persuade libraries with existing legacy applications of the benefits of making these changes in the first place.

Closer to home, the question of how (and how easily) existing systems are able to migrate to the requirements of the new standard will be a key question for libraries to ask of their current or potential suppliers. This will apply not only to RFID suppliers, but equally to LMS providers as well, who will need to be able to show how their systems make use of the standard to enable an interoperable form of interface with RFID.

The AFI (Application Family Identifier)

Agreement on a related, yet separate, element has also been required to enable this standard to work. As RFID tags are now used in many different sectors, a method of differentiating between these sectors is needed to enable systems to function smoothly. For example, a scanner looking for a tag in an airline baggage handling process needs to know that it has found the correct item, despite the possibility that the bag may contain other items – such as library books – that also contain tags.

As mentioned above, the solution to this problem is the Application Family Identifier (AFI), and this is held in a special memory on the tag. There was originally only one AFI for libraries but, in a further development of this concept, there are now two, C2 (hexadecimal) and 07 (hexadecimal).

The benefit of this is that the AFI can then be used as the basis of the security process – where this is the case, then C2 is used for items on loan, and 07 for items on the shelf. (The AFI protocol, again slightly confusingly, currently describes 07 as being for 'in stock' items, but it is clearly meant to distinguish between material that is on loan and that which is not.) The system is then able to discern whether the LMS has issued the item and, if so, changes the status accordingly; if not, the AFI remains unchanged and the tag will trigger the alarm on the security gates. On return, the status is changed back once the item has been discharged.

However, as implied above, the AFI is not the only way of providing the tag with a security function. Suppliers may use another element of the tag for security purposes; this is a simple Electronic Article Surveillance (EAS) bit which is turned on and off accordingly as the item is issued by the system. One of the perceived advantages of the EAS approach is its speed of action as compared with the use of AFI for this purpose, as several items can be read seemingly simultaneously. A disadvantage is that, where a system might otherwise be able to produce a list of items that have triggered an alarm, the use of EAS does not support this.

Again, as with the different approaches to tag encoding, some suppliers offer both solutions within the same system, and leave the choice to the customer. This then becomes simply a question of individual preference, although it should be remembered that the AFI system is now the subject of an agreed approach, incorporated in a standard and therefore interoperable, whereas the EAS method is not.

The DSFID

One final key element on the tag is the Data Storage Format Identifier (DSFID), which tells scanners how the data is stored and so can be used to differentiate between tags coded according to Parts 2 and 3 of ISO 28560.

Summary

The application of RFID in libraries to date has been largely ad hoc and proprietary. The result of this has been that systems have been developed independently, with no attempt to make them interoperable. Libraries have therefore been in danger of buying systems that may become obsolete as suppliers go out of business or change direction. Tags are not useable outside their home library system, and the market for them is fragmented. On the other hand, libraries have been able to choose systems which closely meet their needs. Some library-specific standards are beginning to become available, but their remit is still limited.

Chapter 5

Privacy

Worried about rumours that RFID can compromise individual privacy? Want to know how to use it safely? And – is RFID really the work of the devil?

Interoperability and privacy

Unfortunately, one person's interoperability may be another's invasion of privacy. By making it possible for different systems to communicate with each other, some people fear that the data sharing that may result could produce a 'Big Brother' scenario in which it is all too easy for individuals to be identified, resulting in government snooping, identity theft and other undesirable outcomes.

Such a view has not - so far at least - been very widely held in the UK, or in Europe, although the European Union set up a working party and invited views on the subject in 2005 (European Commission, 2005; Commission of the European Communities, 2007); there was, however, little agreement about the extent of the problem in reality.

This is in marked contrast to the USA - or rather some parts of it - where the use of RFID has been very controversial. In San Francisco, implementation of RFID in libraries has been - and continues to be - the subject of great public debate, while in neighbouring Berkeley it appears to have played a role in the resignation of the chief librarian, Jackie Griffin, from her post (Bender, 2006): 'There have been complaints and protests about the library's radio frequency identification devices, a system Griffin backed and the city spent at least $1.1 million buying and installing. Many library workers have complained about the so-called "spy chips," alleging they compromise patron privacy and deter good customer service.'

RFID opponents

A number of organizations have been very active in trying to alert the public to what they see as the dangers of RFID use in terms of personal liberty, particularly in the post-9/11 scenario of the USA PATRIOT Act and other restrictions on privacy. One of those with the highest profile is CASPIAN (Consumers Against Supermarket Privacy Invasion and Numbering) (www.nocards.org). As is evident from its name, CASPIAN's original concerns stemmed mainly from the use of RFID in the retail world. One of its main targets has been Wal-Mart, which has been at the forefront of RFID use in retail, having mandated its top 100 suppliers to use tags. Wal-Mart's experience has not been entirely unproblematic, with various changes in approach having to be adopted along the way, and some recalcitrant suppliers being fined by them for non-compliance.

It was this early adoption of RFID in retail that alerted CASPIAN to the potential for what it saw as the misuse of this technology. Gillette's linking of RFID and cameras to 'monitor consumer behaviour' when buying razor blades (McCue, 2003) and Benetton's proposed use of RFID to capture consumers' individual preferences (Batista, 2003b) were just two such cases. In the case of razor blades – a comparatively high-value product which can easily be concealed – every person (innocent shoppers and thieves alike) taking them from the display triggered a camera which photographed them in the act of picking them up. Benetton used RFID tags in its clothing products, which then remained live post-sale. If customers returned to the shop wearing the item, scanners then provided shop staff with information about the customer derived from the tag which – in theory at least – would allow them to serve those customers better.

The crucial element in both the Gillette and the Benetton projects is that there appears to have been no attempt to alert customers to either the existence of the technology or the way in which it was being used. CASPIAN says that this is its main concern in these (and other) instances – the surreptitious way in which RFID was applied. Consumers were not alerted to its presence, and the data appeared to be gathered either in a haphazard way, intruding on perfectly respectable shoppers' privacy in an attempt to catch thieves, or else for trivial marketing purposes.

CASPIAN says that its view is that people should be able to make a choice about whether they are exposed to RFID or not. It also says that, rather than seeking legislation to ban RFID, its approach has been to try to ensure that the public are always informed that RFID is in use and are aware of the potential for invasion of privacy. In this way, it hopes that companies will be forced to drop the technology, due to what it believes will be an inevitable decline in business.

Another organization that is similarly concerned about the use of RFID is the Electronic Frontier Foundation (EFF), based in San Francisco. EFF has been particularly involved in campaigning against the use of RFID libraries, and its concerns (EFF, 2004) are that: 'While libraries may be able to use RFIDs to help with the checking in and checking out of books, the technology can also easily be used to track the exact location of those books - and the people who check them out. When books or other expressional materials are "tagged," free speech is also an issue. Libraries have long sought to protect the reading habits of patrons from prying eyes, but RFIDs could drastically undermine that tradition.'

The main trigger for this concern about tracking has been the concept of the 'internet of things' referred to earlier, which - through the use of the unique identifier on a tag registered on the object naming service (ONS) - enables the tag to be traced by anybody with access to the system.

The 'internet of things' concept clearly has much to recommend it to organizations seeking to make major improvements in their supply chain, enabling 'just in time' systems in particular to work to increasingly tighter tolerances. It is also the reason for the great investment being placed in RFID by the USA's Department of Defense, who see the opportunity for both great financial savings and improvements in efficiency.

However, any breach in the security of such systems could make it possible to identify an individual's use of specific products very easily. In addition to the retail examples already referred to, there have been reports in the UK of the use of London Underground Oyster cards in divorce cases, identifying that spouses have not been where they claimed to be at a particular time (Bloomfield, 2006).

But CASPIAN also has been alarmed by the growth of RFID in libraries, although its concerns (and those of the EFF) are less to do with what RFID makes possible in libraries currently, and more with what might be feasible in the future as the technology develops. The limited read distances of the 13.56 MHz tag prevent any meaningful surveillance of individuals at the moment, but CASPIAN fears that this may change and that remote tracking of library books (and therefore of the people who borrow them) via satellite may become a reality in the near future.

In fact, the read distance limitations are not a function solely of the tag but rather of the tag and scanner combined, and so it is (just) possible to envisage a situation in future where scanners are improved to the extent that read distances of 13.56 MHz tags could be lengthened. However, the physics involved in doing so still suggests that this is unlikely in the foreseeable future.

CASPIAN nevertheless contends that any personal data held on a tag – whether in a book or a library card – could be susceptible to being used in ways that the person concerned might not want. Other information – not currently thought to be sensitive – might also be retrievable remotely in a context that might change that assessment. For example, in most circumstances it might be thought harmless for a book tag to include its ISBN (which is proposed for use by booksellers as the basis of the EPCGlobal number, and so would be registered on the 'internet of things') but if it is possible for it to be decoded and for conclusions to be drawn about an individual's reading habits, then the situation suddenly changes.

Hotlisting and tracking

These concerns may appear to be unlikely to be realized in everyday life. However, there are various activities that have become sufficiently widespread to have earned a place in privacy terminology, and which concern privacy organizations in this regard. At their simplest, these include 'skimming', which refers to reading data on a tag without the owner's knowledge or consent by means of an unauthorized scanner; and 'eavesdropping', which is similar but involves the opportunistic interception of the messages being relayed between an authorized reader and a tag.

Each of these understandably concerns privacy organizations, but there are other activities which develop these ideas further, whose potential application to libraries they find particularly worrying:

- 'Hotlisting', in a library context, involves the creation of a database of specific books and their tag numbers, and then - via unauthorized access to an LMS - the identification of the users of those items.
- 'Tracking', as the name implies, uses multiple separate readings to track the movement of an item.

By combining hotlisting and tracking, it would be possible to identify the movement of users of specific titles.

While the existence of an 'internet of things' as proposed by EPCGlobal makes - at least theoretically - the danger of such a scenario more likely in the retail world than in libraries, it might be argued that the increasing development of electronic union catalogues also provides potential support for this kind of activity. OCLC's WorldCat, for example, while having the benign aim of continually improving worldwide access to resources - currently listing over a billion items in 470 different languages held by 69,000 libraries - could be seen by those with privacy concerns simply to confirm all of their worst fears about the ease with which details of specific titles can be found by those with malign intent.

While it is possible to understand the basis of these concerns, it still requires illegal 'hacking' of an LMS for either hotlisting or tracking to succeed - in which case, it might reasonably be argued that the involvement of RFID is, to a large extent, incidental. However, it might equally be argued that RFID's lack of need for line of sight makes it much easier to achieve this outcome surreptitiously.

However, that too is debatable. Nevertheless, the capacity for RFID to carry a range of more meaningful information on the tag does mean that libraries that adopt this approach may wish to review their arrangements. However, those that are less convinced by arguments that RFID opens up all these potential danger areas point out that by far the easiest way to determine what somebody is reading remains straightforward observation.

RFID and (some) religious groups

To most European eyes, at least, some of the more extreme output from organizations such as CASPIAN and EFF does little to foster credibility for their cause. For example, there are a number of claims that RFID is, literally, the work of the devil, of which this (Kravets, 2008) is a comparatively mild example: 'A group of community farmers, some of them Amish, are challenging rules requiring the tagging of livestock with RFID chips, saying the devices are a "mark of the beast." The suit mentions various verses from the Book of Revelation. "He causes all, both small and great, rich and poor, free and slave, to receive a mark on their right hand or on their foreheads, and that no one may buy or sell except one who has the mark or the name of the beast, or the number of his name." Revelation 13: 16–17'.

'GodTube' (www.godtube.com) is a 'family-friendly Christian social network' based in the USA, similar in format to 'YouTube', which has over 60 video clips devoted to demonstrating the links between RFID and the devil.

However, in addition to her work with CASPIAN, Katharine Albrecht is perhaps the best-known individual proponent of such views. Albrecht, together with her colleague Liz McIntyre, has published two very similar books – the first is entitled *Spychips: how major corporations and government plan to track your every move with RFID*, which covers much of the ground ascribed to CASPIAN above. However, the second, *The Spychips Threat: why Christians should resist RFID and electronic surveillance*, places more emphasis on the similarities between RFID and the remarks in Revelation.

RFID and hacking

The effect of such suggestions may be to make library managers feel sanguine about the privacy problems relating to their particular use of RFID.

However, a widely cited paper (Molnar and Wagner, 2004) provides no comfort in this respect: 'Current library RFID tags do not prevent unauthorized reading of tag data . . . both tracking and hotlisting are possible whenever a static identifier is used . . . static identifiers may include collision IDs that are not protected by access control mechanisms intended to protect tag data.'

RFID suppliers have been quick to explain why libraries are not as insecure as this paper suggests. Vinod Chacra and Dennis McPherson (2003) of VTLS have argued that:

- libraries use passive tags, which are less likely to be able to be read remotely
- library tags have a very short read range
- the data stored on library tags have no important personal information
- the LMS database is a more likely source of privacy problems.

Nevertheless, Molnar and Wagner's paper has been followed by many others – again, mainly in the USA – taking a similar line, suggesting that libraries, with their keen desire to protect the privacy of their users, should be the last organizations to use this technology, rather than being at the forefront.

Scott Muir of Arizona State University (Muir, 2007) goes so far as to suggest that, in light of (what appears to be) an escalating concern over patron privacy, use of RFID in libraries warrants further review: 'Given the current limitations, additional libraries may wish to delay implementing RFID systems until some important changes are made to RFID security . . . . Those libraries that decide to move ahead with an RFID implementation should proceed in a very open environment with input from their community.'

The countervailing argument by proponents of RFID use is not helped by other, more publicly apparent examples of RFID seemingly being used in a less than secure way: various scare stories about the potentially insecure nature of the technology surface from time to time – 'Computer viruses could be about to take a giant leap and start spreading via smart barcodes, warn experts' (Ward, 2006) – while others detail real-life examples: 'Dutch scientists have discovered that a certain type of smartcard,

Mifare, which is used to gain access to government departments, schools and hospitals around Britain, is carrying a serious security flaw that allows it to be easily copied. The same Mifare technology is also used for 17 million Oyster cards for travel in London' (Miller, 2008). By intercepting communication between an Oyster card and a scanner (eavesdropping), and using the information to reverse-engineer the Mifare algorithm, credit could be loaded back onto a card to provide free travel. Whether coincidentally or not, the Mayor of London's office announced the same week that the contract for the supply of the Oyster card was being cancelled early, and placed with a different company.

RFID and legal limitations

All of this has, not surprisingly, led to a number of attempts to control – or in some cases prohibit – RFID by legislation: in California, Senator Joe Simitian of Palo Alto proposed a bill (SB 628) that would have banned the use of RFID in official personal documents such as driving licences, as well as the surreptitious interception of RFID signals. Although it was initially passed by the Assembly, it was agreed to postpone it in response to heavy lobbying by representatives of the electronics industry, who pointed out that the US State Department was coincidentally planning to use RFID in passports, as well as drawing up standards for its use in state-issued documents, and that work was under way to improve security and privacy safeguards.

In light of these concerns, some organizations have undertaken work to highlight steps that can be taken to minimize exposure to risks. For example, the Book Industry Study Group (2004) has drawn up guidelines, endorsed by the American Library Association, regarding the management of data in library RFID systems. The basic principles are:

> All businesses, organizations, libraries, educational institutions and non-profits that buy, sell, loan, or otherwise make available books and other content to the public utilizing RFID technologies shall:
>
> ■ Implement and enforce an up-to-date organizational privacy policy that gives notice and full disclosure as to the use, terms of use, and any change in the terms of use for data collected

via new technologies and processes, including RFID.

■ Ensure that no personal information is recorded on RFID tags which, however, may contain a variety of transactional data.

■ Protect data by reasonable security safeguards against interpretation by any unauthorized third party.

■ Comply with relevant federal, state, and local laws as well as industry best practices and policies.

■ Ensure that the four principles outlined above must be verifiable by an independent audit.

Other organizations, such as Ontario Public Libraries in Canada, have produced similar guidance (Cavoukian, 2004). While accepting that the technology is changing quickly, they suggest that 'Future challenges are difficult to foresee but implementing the above guidelines will help to provide libraries with fundamental security and privacy protections, complementing the benefits that RFID technology provides.'

As noted above, there are already some protections available in the existing technology – the fact that tags used by libraries are passive rather than active, for example, and the limited read range of 13.56 MHz tags. Some have also suggested that encryption may be a solution; however, this is something which seems to be discussed more than actively pursued, in the library world at least.

Encrypted tags?

The limited availability of encrypted tags appears to be due to the fact that encryption is both difficult and expensive to achieve. Kelsey Livingston and Jennifer Tam (n.d.) demonstrate the difficulty of the problems faced – how do you deliver the key message without displaying it at the same time – as well as the current weaknesses of the various protocols, while Olga Kharif (2006) suggests that while some tags have recently been developed with more secure chips, this improvement comes at a price which is both financial (they cost $4, as compared with the more usual 20 cents) and practical (the read range is reduced to a few centimetres to make surreptitious reading more difficult).

RFID and privacy – a continuing debate

It is nevertheless clear that – in some parts of the world at least – the question of privacy will continue to be a prime concern: perhaps unsurprisingly, a recent US title providing guidance to librarians on privacy in the electronic world (Woodward, 2007) contains an entire chapter on, and many other references to, RFID. However, while such concerns about privacy are understandable, it can also be argued that the public make decisions about the balance between the risks and benefits of technology all the time – albeit often without realizing. The extraordinary growth in use of mobile phones since the early 1990s suggests that users are either unworried or unaware that their whereabouts can be traced very precisely every time they make a call or send a text. With the ready and cheap availability of services now offering to track individuals in this way, it may be that privacy concerns will surface belatedly in this area, but it seems unlikely that many people will surrender the convenience and accessibility provided by mobile phones for such a reason.

Whether the public views the ease of use of libraries provided by RFID in the same way is a moot point, but there is clearly an obligation on the part of library managers to ensure that no personal information is open to abuse as a result of using RFID, by adopting approaches such as those outlined in the guidelines referred to above.

Summary

The relationship between RFID and privacy is contentious in some parts of the world: the move to interoperability may make this more of a problem. However, the limitations of RFID employed at the frequencies currently used by libraries mean that most of these claims are difficult to realise using existing technology. Nevertheless, libraries need to ensure that no personal information is held on tags, and that personal data held on the LMS remains secure.

Chapter 6

RFID and health and safety

Is RFID is safe? How can you tell? What laws and standards are there?

RFID - what are the safety concerns?

While concerns about privacy may not be universally held it might be expected that the health and safety implications of RFID would be an area of common interest to all potential users.

This is certainly true, albeit at a fairly specific level. Understandably, any technology which exposes its users to an additional source of electro-magnetic radiation, which is the basis of RFID - even at very low levels - is likely to be the subject of a certain amount of legislation and regulation. Anxiety over prolonged use of mobile phones, for example, which also produce electromagnetic radiation, has shown that - despite regulation - there are many members of the public who remain unconvinced of the safety of prolonged use of such devices.

RFID and health and safety law

The legal position, in Europe at least, is in a transitional phase. The European Union published its Physical Agents (Electromagnetic Fields)

Directive (2004/40/EC) in April 2004, at which point it came into force but with a target date of 30 April 2008 for completion of implementation by all Member States. However, this date was amended to 2012 in light of further research which suggested that some procedures in the medical field might exceed the directive's recommendations. Further research is now being undertaken so that any necessary amendments can be introduced before the 2012 deadline.

Nevertheless, the main areas of concern of the legislation are clear from the original directive, and relate to the possible risks of the exposure of workers to electromagnetic fields – primarily from short-term exposure to induced currents, energy absorption and contact currents. It outlines the minimum requirements necessary to address potential problems arising from these elements, but does not attempt to cover possible longer-term problems.

The limits to exposure that the directive stipulates are based on work carried out previously by the International Commission on Non-Ionizing Radiation Protection (ICNIRP) (see www.icnirp.org), an independent organization that has done extensive research in this field.

However, it should be noted that this is the European position only, and that the legal situation will be different around the world. While many governments use the ICNIRP work as a basis for legislation, the ways in which RFID is implemented internationally nevertheless vary considerably. This is because governments are responsible for the allocation of frequencies within their country: this covers not only the areas of the frequency spectrum that are made available, but also the power at which they can be used.

For example, in Japan it has only recently become possible to use RFID at UHF frequencies, although it is now being taken up rapidly. There are also differences in the way UHF has been adopted in the USA as compared with Europe, and although work is under way to harmonize these systems so that tags produced for use in the USA will work satisfactorily within Europe, this will be at the cost of a reduction in read range of 10%.

These differences in national regulations explain why some features of RFID use in libraries are not common to all, with certain aspects of library installations in some countries not feasible in others, reflecting the different regulatory environments.

Which standards?

Despite these international differences, there is one standard to which RFID suppliers usually refer when wishing to reassure their customers that their equipment satisfies health and safety requirements. IEEE C.95-1-1991 (Institute of Electrical and Electronics Engineers, 1991) provides the currently accepted standard for safety levels for human exposure to RF electromagnetic fields. RFID suppliers will understandably emphasize that their systems generally (at least those at sub-microwave level), and certainly those used in libraries, fall far below the limits set by this regulation. They will also point out that power levels and exposure times are significantly lower (for staff and for customers) than those for mobile phones, for example.

RFID and medical devices?

Another aspect that is frequently queried is the effect that RFID might have on pacemakers and similar medical devices, and again suppliers can point to the fact that the normal power output of RFID systems is too low to affect them. What is more, modern pacemakers, implantable cardioverter defibrillators and other similar devices have also had to have their resistance to RF interference significantly improved precisely because of problems caused by the massive growth in use of mobile phones. Similarly, the fact that RFID is heavily used in hospitals to manage the location and retrieval of equipment further suggests that it should not have a negative effect on health.

RFID and health and safety – the plus side?

There are, of course, some positive aspects claimed for RFID in terms of health and safety – the main one being fewer instances of repetitive strain injury (RSI) among staff, as they have to handle books less frequently and usually in less constrained circumstances. Other aspects include the creation of more interesting and less tedious tasks for staff, freed from the need to perform routine counter duties, and so resulting in more enjoyable and less stressful time at work.

RFID and health and safety – the future?

Nevertheless, current legislation and regulations are seen by some as providing only comparatively limited reassurance. Some industry observers contend that there will eventually have to be far more regulation of devices that make use of electromagnetic radiation – not only because of, but obviously partly due to, concerns about mobile phones in particular – and also note that the technology is continually evolving. ICNIRP's statement (2004) on the effects of exposure to electromagnetic fields associated with the use of electronic security devices (both RF and RFID) suggests that further work should be undertaken to improve the health risk assessment of these devices.

Similarly, the UK's Health and Safety Executive has produced a horizon-scanning document (HSE, 2007) which summarizes the current situation as follows:

> Manufacturers of RFID systems argue that as the power levels and exposure times of the transmissions between the readers and tags are relatively low, compared with mobile phones for example, then the associated health & safety risks are also low. This may well be the case but studies to date appear to provide little definitive evidence to either support or challenge this view . . . .The extent to which RFID systems represent a significant occupational risk in terms of exposure to electromagnetic radiation and other hazards . . . are as yet unclear and may warrant more in-depth investigation.

Summary

So, it is probable that current legislation will both change and become more comprehensive in light of the findings of any such further investigations, but currently IEEE C.95-1-1991 is the primary standard with which RFID has to conform.

Chapter 7

RFID and library design

How can RFID influence library layouts? Does RFID affect work areas too?

The changing role of library buildings

Library buildings have to accommodate a remarkable, and occasionally unreasonable, range of demand. Increasingly, this is a result of a desire for them to be, or be part of, multipurpose community hubs, one-stop shops, or satellite outreach facilities, aimed at audiences who might otherwise never think of going to a library, or who are unable to access the service in any other way.

This places further pressure on the manager seeking to maximize the use of what is often already inadequate space for library stock and staff, but is only the latest in a long series of challenges facing those charged with designing library spaces.

Godfrey Thompson's detailed and pragmatic guide to library design (1989) makes it clear that the responsibility of planning a building intended to be adaptable to all of the changes likely over the next 60 years has always been a heavy one. Sometimes, this is because of the competing requirements of the architect, wishing to produce a building that makes a 'statement', and of the librarian, who may sympathize with the architect's objectives but hopes that it will nevertheless still be possible to change the light bulbs without having to hire tower scaffolding.

Such situations are not uncommon, and have been a feature of library design since the two professions began working together. However, the challenges created by changing technology and demand are currently both more pressing and fundamental. Thompson's design guide was first published in 1973, but by the time of its third edition in 1989 computerization had begun to have a significant and disruptive influence on library planning.

The impact of computerization

Some of this was perceived as beneficial: electronic union catalogues not only gave library users much better service - customers were no longer limited to the resources of the building they were in; they could see at a glance whether what they sought was immediately available; and if not they could instantly place a reservation - but they also did away with the need to find space to accommodate thousands of 5 x 3 cards. Not only that, but as users became more familiar with computers (and as library catalogues became less proprietary and more mainstream), the location of public access terminals became less dependent on the ready availability of staff to provide tuition in their use, and they could be more freely distributed around the library.

Similarly, automated library management systems also had the potential to reduce the size of library counters, previously required to hold the library's entire current lending transactions in the form of individual cardboard tickets and cards. Admittedly, some of this newly gained space was soon lost again to the health and safety requirements for use of visual display screens, but the electronic storage of the actual loan and return transactions nevertheless provided an opportunity (and an obligation) to rethink the design of library counters.

However, the increasing availability and capabilities of computers had also begun to raise more fundamental questions about library design, not the least of which was - would traditional, bound paper books still be in common use in 60 or so years' time, and if not, why would a building be required to house them? This question remains unresolved: generations of e-book reading devices have come and gone, although Amazon's Kindle and Sony's e-reader – at the time of writing the two latest and most successful proprietary e-book readers (and, perhaps more significantly in the longer term, the use of Apple's iPhone and iPod Touch as platforms for reading) – have seen a huge increase in the downloading of books from the internet.

Perhaps even more relevant in this context is the development of 'Second Life' activity, in both academic and public libraries. This multi-user, virtual, environment has seen huge growth in a very short time, with millions of users accessing digital information provided by librarians around the world in a context that brings together the two previously (mainly) discrete worlds of education and gaming.

Consequently, any manager contemplating a new library building may feel that even the two main staples of library design have suddenly become less of a 'given' – if virtual reference means there is no need for an enquiry desk, and e-books mean there is no need for miles of shelving, what remains?

However, despite these developments, no serious commentators have suggested that the end of the traditional book is likely to occur in the foreseeable future (although the same may not be entirely true for printed journals in academic libraries). Consequently, the challenge facing most library designers in the early 21st century is how to accommodate all of these competing demands – a hybrid library that offers books and electronic resources, space for community activity and individual study, coffee shops and quiet areas, children's story times and access to local history, and much more.

Such a concept has much in common with the idea of the 'Third Place' popularized by Ray Oldenberg (1989), in which the 'first place' – home – and the 'second place' – work – are complemented by a 'third place', a community resource where individuals and families can regularly meet on shared or neutral ground which is free (or cheap) and easily accessible. Most library workers would argue that this is precisely the function that libraries of all kinds have always fulfilled, and that – even if this role has been largely invisible to non-library users and, often, to the parent organizations responsible for library provision – this broader social purpose places libraries squarely at the centre of community engagement and cohesion, whether in public or academic settings.

Moreover, this hypothesis argues that this role does not compete with what some see as the library's primary (if not only) purpose of providing books and information, but is in fact a *sine qua non* of that role. Like Sir Philip Sydney's ideal poetry, which has both to teach and delight in order to be successful – and if it does not do both does neither effectively – libraries with perfect collections of material but no audience, or with highly effective community engagement but no material will both fail to fulfil their potential in different ways.

There are many examples of this approach around the world – it forms one of the main planks of the UK government's 'blueprint' for public libraries, *Framework for the Future* (DCMS, 2003); in the USA, of Chicago's 'engaged library' (Urban Libraries Council, 2006); and in New Zealand, Christchurch's initiative to link libraries to the city's community outcomes (Moen, 2006).

The idea of the 'third place' however, has also provided the public library in particular with unlooked-for competition. Already faced with a fierce challenge to two of its previous near monopolies – the provision of free loans of books by increasingly cheaper outlets such as online suppliers and supermarkets; and of free information by the internet – in many areas the public library also finds its claim to be the 'third place' usurped by commercial organizations such as coffee shops and bookshops, or more often a combination of the two. Starbucks, for example, has not only entered into joint arrangements with bookshops (Barnes and Noble in the USA, Borders in the UK), but has actively marketed itself as the 'third place' in which to spend time away from home or work.

What's this got to do with RFID?

Although RFID is unable to provide a tailored solution to each of these challenges, it can at least offer the next best thing – flexibility of approach. This can enable library designers to maximize the opportunities provided by their buildings to fulfil each of these roles in ways which make sense to – and attract – audiences accustomed to sophisticated retail techniques and the latest technology, without alienating more traditional clientele. Which is not to say that it is easy to achieve – simply that it provides an opportunity to look at things in a different way.

Library layout

Library layouts have to reconcile a number of often competing requirements, essentially the relationships between 'functional', 'auxiliary' and 'circulation' spaces. The auxiliary space – those areas that are taken up by heating, ventilation and other infrastructure – is effectively determined by the technologies available at the time of design and is unlikely to change (at least, not without significant expense) during the lifetime of the building. However, the balance between the functional and circulation requirements is more open to adjustment, and the opportunities made available by RFID can shift this significantly.

Traditionally, two of the key elements in the design of library layouts have been the issue/return counter and the enquiry desk. Additionally, the counter's size and location have frequently been a predeterminant of everything else in the library. As a result, the counter has usually been the focus of a great amount of thought – not because of the range of activity undertaken there, which is comparatively limited, but because of the importance and frequency of those activities. The processes for the fundamental activity of a lending library – the borrowing and returning of material – need to be transparent to the user, and so the placing of the counter at a key focal point in the building has always been crucial. This is further reinforced where security systems have been introduced, as the relationship between the counter and the security gates is often – and, in the case of by-pass systems, completely – critical.

RFID subverts this traditional position by doing away with the need for a counter at all – at least in theory, or indeed in practice if a 100% self-service approach is adopted. This means, in turn, that the focus of attention has to transfer to the location of the self-service equipment, as the need for the process to be transparent to the user remains. Nevertheless, it also does two other important things. Firstly, as the self-service units are almost always smaller than the counter, it frees up space that can be used for more customer-friendly purposes; secondly, and perhaps more significantly, it removes the staffing element from the loan/return process.

As demonstrated later in Chapters 9 and 12, this offers the opportunity for the staff role to change fundamentally from being a transaction-based one to one that is more flexible and customer oriented. However, it also changes the ways in which the staff are able to control the building, as they are no longer tied to one particular area. It consequently begins to blur the traditional distinction between 'functional' and 'circulation' areas, since customer/staff interaction can take occur in either.

This merging of space can also be applied to the information function of the library, by exploiting other technological changes: as with the issue/return counter, the traditional enquiry desk begins to look redundant in a world where many, if not most, reference sources are electronic and access to them can be provided from almost anywhere in the building, either through distributed online terminals or, more likely, wireless networks. When mobile communication technology is added to the mix, again freeing staff from the confines of a fixed workstation, then again the functional/circulation distinction becomes less clear cut.

This approach can be seen in both public and academic libraries – in the latter case, JISC's guide, *Designing Spaces for Effective Learning* (2006), is imbued throughout with the concept, although it also makes it clear that other problems then have to be taken into account: it describes a 'self-regulating building' which demonstrates 'a more sophisticated understanding of space management, where sound and visual clues, layout and style of furniture, and different types of technology in different configurations, signal the different purposes of areas in the centres [and] . . . an ethos of partnership between learners and administrators, shown by the avoidance of external controls . . .'.

However, it points out that the management of noise then becomes crucial to the success of the building: 'the self-regulating building will manage dialogue and collaboration by providing areas that invite group activities where silence is not expected, with quiet zones adjacent to windows, or separated by shelving . . .'.

While clearly of great benefit to library planners and managers, however, a lack of clear demarcation between public and staff areas may well be viewed rather differently by the library staff, who have to make the layout work. Deprived of both a defined workspace and any barrier between them and their customers, it would not be surprising if some staff were to feel vulnerable at the very least, and in more extreme cases, threatened by the lack of a formal area in which to work. Consequently, the early provision of staff development and support clearly becomes even more important.

Library furniture
For staff

The redefinition of work processes made possible by RFID has meant, as already noted, far less reliance on the counter as a workstation, as the emphasis for staff tends to focus much more on floor walking and closer interaction with customers. In some cases this may mean the complete removal of the counter, while in others it results in a much smaller unit being introduced as a replacement. Where smaller units are deployed, however, care must be taken to ensure that they still adhere to all health and safety requirements for flexibility and ergonomics.

In smaller libraries, in particular, the nature of working patterns needs also to be taken into account: a combination of limited behind-the-scenes space and reduced staff flexibility will often mean that work which would be done in a workroom in larger libraries will need to be carried out in the library. As a result, it will be difficult to reduce the size of staff workstations significantly without impinging on the space required to do this kind of work. It may be possible to cater for this through the use of work surfaces that can be folded away until needed, or similar means, but this will need careful design.

For the customer
Self-service units

Most RFID suppliers provide a choice of standard furniture to house their self-service equipment, although there will often be a choice regarding specific features, particularly if the units are single purpose – e.g. self-issue or self-return only – rather than multipurpose. Some suppliers emphasize that their equipment is compatible with a wide range of furniture styles, which may be independently commissioned by the library.

Bins, shelves or trolleys?

One fundamental decision that will have to be made is whether simply to have shelving or trolleys available on which customers can place returned material, or to use bins to provide more security. Similarly – assuming the system deals with exceptions – a decision will have to be made regarding where customers are instructed to place requests and similar material. The use of bins is one of the most common approaches to dealing with exceptions and, although far from foolproof, works sufficiently well in most circumstances. Alternative approaches – such as asking the customer to take the item to a member of staff, or to have a separate shelving area for requests – seem a less than secure way of dealing with in-demand material.

Some libraries store all their returns in bins, having one for exceptions and another for everything else. This helps to provide the customer with a sense of security, but creates extra work for the staff, as the bins then have to be emptied and their contents transferred to trolleys prior to reshelving. It also means there is a delay in items becoming available again for loan, contradicting most of the principles of reader development and customer care generally.

Security and building supervision

One effect of this change in staff role that is sometimes overlooked is the way in which it opens up the possibility of more effective supervision of the building. Instead of having to rely primarily on security tags or closed-circuit television (or dedicated security staff, in larger buildings) as a deterrent to potential thieves, the increased presence of staff around the building, rather than their being confined to the counter area, can enhance the safety of both stock and customers.

Statistics from the retail world indicate that this extra level of security can have a significant effect. Although not universally admired, Wal-Mart's greeters are recognized as performing a function over and above simply saying 'hello' and providing basic assistance. As noted in an article providing guidance to booksellers in how to avoid 'shrinkage' (Randall, 2006), Wal-Mart also found that 'shoplifting was reduced in their superstores by as much as 35% . . . it seems that thieves loathe bookshops with friendly, attentive staff. Eye contact is the essential component.'

External aspects

RFID is also able to provide an out-of-hours book return facility. While many libraries make use of book-drops or even simply letter boxes to enable customers to return items after the library has closed, this is still dependent on the book being eventually discharged by a member of staff. RFID return chutes, on the other hand, are able to register the return immediately through their links to the LMS, and so provide an improved service to the customer.

This may require the library to review its policies regarding charges for the late return of material, and also the settings on its LMS: if late return is deemed to mean 'returned after the library has closed', then a charge will still be applicable even if the chute is used. However, if return is allowed until midnight on the due date, then charges would not be applicable.

Although one of the early selling points for RFID in libraries, the use of external chutes to cater for out-of-hours returns is not as widespread as it might be. This is partly to do with the cost and difficulties experienced in getting chutes to work as intended, but equally many libraries find that they simply do not have an appropriate wall, with enough space behind it, to accommodate such a device.

Summary

RFID has the potential to support significant change in the design of libraries, including moves to new uses of library space for community activity. It is particularly useful in altering the balance between functional and circulation space. However, the implications for design of furniture and equipment, as well as the effects on staff, need to be carefully thought through.

Chapter 8

Building a business case for RFID in libraries, and requesting proposals

What are you going use RFID for? How are you going to pay for it? Why are you doing it? What are you going to ask for?

Risk and reward

Most libraries contemplating the introduction of RFID – as with any other initiative – will probably require a business case to demonstrate:

■ the rationale for wanting to move in this direction
■ what alternatives exist
■ how the technology will be used
■ the implications for staffing
■ what might constitute a return on investment
■ how this return might be achieved
■ the risks involved, both in adopting RFID and in not adopting it.

Rationale

Libraries may wish to implement RFID for a variety of reasons: in some cases, they may be seeking to resolve problems with a specific building or element of service, while in others it may simply be a desire to modernize the service.

However, the overarching theme in most cases will probably be a desire to provide better customer service, whether through simpler and quicker transaction processes, longer opening hours, or improved stock management.

This in turn begins to define the applications for which RFID will be used – self-service, supply chain management, stock security and stocktaking, and so on.

Implementing RFID – the benefits

As we have seen, the main impetus behind the rapid adoption of RFID in libraries has been much less about the technology itself, and much more about what can be done with it. However, this also implies that there is much more that has to be done with it to achieve a useful outcome.

It would be perfectly possible simply to install RFID and sit back and wait for the benefits. Possible, but not advisable, as this implies a level of technological determinism that even Veblen might have found extreme. Installing a new technology like RFID cannot, by itself, provide a solution to all existing problems while automatically realizing all the benefits. Unless all of the processes affected have been thoroughly analysed beforehand, there is a strong likelihood that RFID will simply magnify all the shortcomings of the original approach, and none of the potential benefits will be found.

As Paul Strassman (1996) has consistently stated since his initial investigations of the value of computerization in the 1980s: 'It is unlikely that any direct relationship between computerization and profitability can be ever demonstrated. Computers are only catalysts. Business value is created by well organized, well motivated and knowledgeable people . . . .'

In this light, RFID – particularly the self-service element – provides the opportunity to completely rethink service delivery in a way that meets customer needs much more flexibly, and which is much more attuned to the demands of the early 21st century. Although this obviously impacts on the basic transactional business of the library, it can – and should – be much more pervasive, affecting most, if not all, aspects of the service.

Staff roles and job profiles; staff development; stock presentation; service branding – all of these need to be interlinked in a holistic approach if the full benefits of RFID are to be realized.

Figure 8.1 illustrates how a major RFID project can be placed at the centre of the strategic management of a library service.

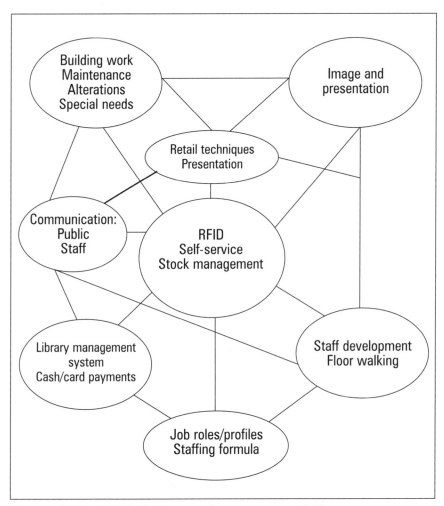

Figure 8.1   RFID links to other aspects of library management

Putting this into practice is not easy, but a checklist produced by the BIC/CILIP RFID in Libraries Group in 2005 provides a framework for doing so, and begins by asking some key questions that need to be addressed even before starting along the RFID route:

- How will RFID improve customer service?
- What will RFID be used for?
- Does the library have a parent organization that has to be consulted?
- How will RFID affect staffing and procedures?
- How will return in investment be calculated?
- How will RFID work with the library management system?
- What criteria will be used to choose an RFID system?
- What timeframe will be needed for implementation?
- What support and maintenance will be needed, and provided?
- Are there any data protection issues?
- How will RFID be promoted?
- How will the success of RFID be measured and monitored?

Each of these and other questions is explored more fully below.

How will RFID improve customer service?

Will RFID be used as part of an overarching project, incorporating new ways of presenting the service, for example through extended opening hours, aids to navigating the building, new methods of stock arrangement, or similar?

Which RFID applications will be employed?

- Self-issue
- Self-return
- Security
- External book drops/chutes
- Hand-held devices for stock management and/or for the public
- Smart shelves
- Supply chain
- Something else?

Will RFID be used in conjunction with other technologies, such as self-service payment?

If it is, who will provide these other technologies, and who will be responsible for making them work with the RFID system? How will it link to the LMS and the charges it raises? Will it be compatible with credit and debit cards?

What will RFID be used for?

Will RFID tags be used only for stock - and if so, will this include all material, or only books? If they are to be used for audiovisual material, how will the limitations of tag performance when used with CDs and DVDs be dealt with? Will they be used for sets of material, and if so, how will the different set parts be dealt with?

Alternatively, will RFID also be used for library membership cards, and if so will the cards include a cash facility, such as an electronic purse? Is it possible to incorporate smart cards that may already be in use by a partner or parent organization - for example, access cards used on a university campus, or the Oyster travel card used in London? If so, who will own the card?

Does the library have a parent organization that has to be consulted?

It is unlikely that many libraries will be entirely autonomous, and most will need to have regard for the arrangements and policies that their parent organization - whether a local authority, academic institution or private firm - may have regarding ICT, procurement, human resources, finance and similar core services.

How will RFID affect staffing and procedures?

Will library staff continue fulfilling the same roles as before? If not, what will they be doing? Close and timely consultation with trade unions and other staff groups will probably be necessary (and advisable) if significant changes are expected. If one of the major perceived benefits of RFID for many libraries is the possibility of freeing staff from routine counter duties, then what are they being freed to do and how are they going to be supported in making that transition?

Equally important will be the need to review processes. Although this may seem obvious, the danger of simply automating existing procedures rather than undertaking a fundamental re-engineering of processes is that the full benefits of the technology may never be realized. The possibly apocryphal story of a consultant's experience when working with the British Army to improve efficiency illustrates how easy it is to accept the status quo: when working with an artillery gun squad he noticed that, although the team consisted of six gunners, there appeared to be sufficient work for only five of them. When he enquired why this was, nobody was able to explain and it was only after further investigation it was found that the sixth man's role was to hold the horses – many years after they had been replaced by a modern form of horsepower.

While changes in role relating to counter duties may be expected following the introduction of self-service, the use of RFID for stock management may also require some rethinking of the processes associated specifically with that aspect of work. Indeed, many libraries may not have undertaken an inventory process in recent years, or at all, due to the staff-intensive nature of the work or the inability to close for any extended period.

Similarly, automated stock editing using hand-held devices may need staff to make decisions about individual stock items that they are not entirely comfortable about, and so additional training and guidelines may be necessary.

How will return on investment be calculated?

The preparation of a business case seems to presuppose that a quantifiable return on investment will be achieved. However, some libraries may not approach RFID in this light at all. For example, in the UK Cornwall County Library service, whose RFID implementation won the second BIC/CILIP Award for RFID in Libraries in 2008, had a much simpler rationale. It argued that it was unable to maintain its current network of libraries within its existing budget, and that the introduction of self-service was essential if library closures were to be avoided.

Clearly, there was still a quantifiable outcome to this project – the network of libraries was able to be maintained within existing funding levels – but the return on investment was not simply a cashable benefit.

This mix of cashable and non-cashable outcomes is a useful way of approaching a business plan for RFID in libraries. Nevertheless, cashable benefits are usually the main focus of many RFID projects, and the return on investment from RFID implementation is often represented in a fairly straightforward way. This approach emphasizes the freeing of staff time that should follow from the introduction of self-service, and which produces a tangible outcome that can be used to calculate savings at an early stage. Indeed, at least one RFID system supplier provides an ROI calculator to help to do this (www.intellident.co.uk/en/4.00/sm_librariesROI.php).

However, staff savings can be used in more than one way: clearly, they can be realized simply to make financial savings, as suggested above. Alternatively, they can be reinvested in the service, either to fund other developments or to enable the staff to be redeployed to other, more valuable purposes. See Chapter 9 for more on this.

Clearly, most of these elements will be fundamental to most libraries' business cases. However, there are also some benefits that can be gained from RFID introduction that cannot be easily achieved in any other way, and they should not be lost sight of.

These include step changes in the way in the library presents its stock and more flexible use of the library building, but also the introduction of services and processes which would be simply too staff intensive to contemplate otherwise. The most obvious of these is stocktaking, which most libraries have been increasingly unable to make a very high priority, due to the combination of staff time and the level of service downtime required to achieve it.

The Vatican Library is perhaps the best example of this, where, prior to the adoption of RFID, stocktaking required the library to close for a month each year. With hand-held scanners, this is no longer necessary as the work can be done in a matter of hours, with a consequent reduction in downtime and an improved success rate in finding items.

This kind of gain in efficiency and effectiveness can be difficult to quantify, however, and for this reason can sometimes be relegated to a comparatively low priority in a business case, but it can be just as important – if not more so – as the more obvious elements.

In fact, it might be argued that the potential for future service developments that RFID opens up can be so large that it is not possible to place a value on it. Bruce Sterling (1994) in *The Hacker Crackdown*, for example, says that the telephone system in the USA today is unrecognizable from that available in the 1960s as a result of the introduction of computing technology. It has produced a level of service – now expected as the norm – which the old technology could not begin to approach. Most tellingly, he claims that 'computers can handle hundreds of calls per second. Humans simply can't. If every single human being in America worked for the phone company, we couldn't match the performance of digital switches: direct-dialling, three-way calling, speed-calling, call-waiting, Caller ID, all the rest of the cornucopia of digital bounty. Replacing computers with operators is simply not an option anymore.'

Although such a level of technological advantage is unlikely to be gained (or even desired) by libraries using RFID, it does suggest how previously unanticipated new services might become possible in the future, without ever having been part of any original calculation of return on investment.

Self-service

As we have seen, this is the single most popular use of RFID in libraries to date. Even so, RFID is not essential for self-service – it has been available using barcode technology for many years, and continues to be so.

However, the main reason that RFID-based self-service has been taken up so widely is that the evidence suggests that self-service based on barcode technology has generally been less popular with users, with only low levels of take-up. This is not to belittle the achievement of the many libraries that have been able to attain impressive levels of self-service with such systems, but simply to recognize that they have tended to be the exception rather than the rule. A survey by Catherine Snelling (2005) found that most libraries using barcode-based systems achieved self-service levels below 10% of total issues – with self-return not usually featured at all.

How will RFID work with the library management system?

See Chapter 3.

What criteria will be used to choose an RFID system?

While this should be comparatively straightforward to determine, the relative importance of each criterion should be made clear to potential suppliers, and the marking of their responses to tenders should reflect this. See Chapter 10.

What timeframe will be needed for implementation?

This will understandably vary according to the number of sites involved, but one crucial element will certainly be the length of time required to tag all stock – see Chapter 11. Linking this to other external factors, such as school term times or children's summer reading challenges, may well result in a longer implementation period than originally envisaged, especially when the need to coordinate the work of different contractors and suppliers is taken into account.

What support and maintenance will be needed, and provided?

Does the supplier provide support, or is a third party used? What level of support is provided, is it 24/7, and how much does it cost?

Are there any data protection issues?

This is covered in more detail in Chapter 5, but any RFID implementation will obviously have to conform to any existing data protection and privacy policies and laws.

How will RFID be promoted?

Introducing a fundamentally different form of service delivery, particularly one which will probably involve customers as well as staff in having to interact with the library in a completely new way, will need to be promoted very carefully and may involve a wide range of partners, including corporate communications and media departments, who will need to fully understand the implications of all aspects of the project.

How will the success of RFID be measured, and monitored?

What is RFID intended to achieve? How will its success be judged? Will it simply be quantitative – the number of people using it, or the proportion of transactions it accounts for? If so, how will this be measured – will the self-service units themselves provide data, or will it have to be obtained from the LMS? Alternatively, is RFID only part of a wider project, whose success will be measured more qualitatively? If so, by what criteria will the project be judged, and how will RFID's contribution to its success be assessed?

Preparing a request for proposal (RFP)

Detailed consideration of all of these questions should enable library managers to produce a fairly comprehensive specification for their ideal system, suited to their particular requirements. The technical and commercial routes to be followed when seeking a supplier will vary according to the size and value of the potential contract, and also the particular nature of any parent body's procurement arrangements. Whatever they might be, however, it is likely (if not essential) that some kind of tender document or equivalent will be required.

The specification should be constructed to make it as easy as possible for potential suppliers to understand how and why the library is planning to use RFID, and also so that they can show how they might fulfil these requirements. It will need to include full details of the library or libraries involved, ranging from the size and nature of their stock, the level of lending business, and any relevant information that may be specific to each building.

The document needs to make it clear which LMS is currently used, and whether there are any plans to change this. It also needs to specify whether the request is for both hardware and software, and particularly whether the supply of tags forms a part of the contract or whether they will be obtained separately.

Potential suppliers should be asked how they conform to existing standards, and how their systems might adapt to any future changes in standards. Similarly, levels of interoperability should be able to be demonstrated, along with any facilities for self-payment. Libraries should make it clear whether they are also seeking to use RFID library cards.

In addition to specifying details of the proposed system, suppliers should also be asked to indicate how they will support the library service in making the move to RFID, whether by providing practical support such as tagging machines or simply giving advice, but more importantly, in any other conversion work that may be necessary – for example, in rendering any tags used by existing security systems inactive.

However, there is a balance to be struck between being suitably prescriptive about relevant technical and interoperability matters, but still allowing sufficient leeway for the supplier to be able to suggest alternative approaches to particular problems. The best RFPs will not necessarily ask suppliers to provide a technical response to a specific problem, but rather invite them to suggest how their system might avoid the need to address the problem in the first place.

Summary

The most successful RFID installations use the technology as part of a wider initiative rather than as an end in itself, as it offers the opportunity to rethink service delivery from start to finish. This broader context needs to inform the development of the business case, which in turn will determine the ingredients of the request for proposal (RFP). The RFP should specify outcomes rather than inputs, and adherence to standards, but it also needs to provide potential suppliers with sufficient detail of the other systems that RFID will have to work with.

Chapter 9

Staffing: savings, redeployment or something else?

If your staff aren't going to be stamping books, what will they be doing? How many of them will you need?

RFID and staffing efficiencies

One of the main reasons for the popularity of RFID in libraries, as we have seen, has been the popularity of the self-service systems it can provide, resulting in high levels of take-up by the public, and the consequent freeing of staff from routine counter procedures.

As staffing tends to account for the largest single element of most libraries' expenditure, this understandably leads to questions about whether financial savings can be made as a result of this reduction in workload. Different library services have responded to these questions in different ways, reflecting their circumstances and the underlying aims of their business cases. Nevertheless, this topic is usually at the heart of most RFID deployments, with some library services taking 100% of the savings available to them to meet budgetary pressures or efficiency drives, others retaining all the staff time freed and using it for other purposes, or a combination of the two, offering an improvement to the customer but still saving money.

For example, in the UK the approach taken by Essex County Council's Libraries Department when building its business case to roll out RFID beyond its existing four sites was to identify the levels of saving that could be made in staff time, and then show how these could be used to achieve a mix of outcomes. It demonstrated how it could:

■ meet the requirements of the UK government's Gershon agenda for efficiency in public services (a continuous reduction in budgets of 2.5% per annum)
■ repay the cost of the RFID system itself, and also
■ reinvest some of the savings to provide value-added services for library users.

How much work is being saved?

However, although staff savings may be the key to many libraries' business cases, identification of the precise amount of staff time to be saved in each case is not always easy, suppliers' ready reckoners notwithstanding. Most libraries will have staffing schedules that they can analyse, and these will certainly be of help, but those library services that use a detailed staffing formula, based on observation by experienced work study practitioners, will be in a particularly good position to estimate the amount of staff time currently devoted to counter duties.

In fact, one of the main criticisms made of such formulae – that they simply measure workload and do not reflect the staffing that might be required if a fully customer-centred service were provided – becomes a positive advantage since it is precisely workload measurement that is required in this instance. Calculation of the potential savings available, based on the expected level of take-up of self-service, suddenly becomes much easier.

Using staffing formulae

A specific illustration from the Essex approach shows how this can be done. Essex Libraries has a long history of using staffing formulae to determine requirements and levels at each of its sites. It had been an early adopter of the formulae developed by LAMSAC (Local Authorities Management

Services and Computer Committee) for the Department of Education and Science (LAMSAC, 1976), which provided a basis for calculating staffing requirements in a variety of public library settings. Unfortunately, much of this work was based on manual issue systems, and had to be adapted locally following the introduction of computerized LMS. As these systems developed, the formulae had to be continually adapted to accommodate changes to working practice. Eventually, in the early 1990s, Essex Libraries commissioned the county council's management support service to devise an updated approach reflecting current processes.

Like the LAMSAC formula, its replacement also used a modular approach. As the total staffing requirement was made up of individual elements of library work, it was possible to identify the amount of staffing for each library generated by counter duties. Table 9.1 shows the outcome of applying the formula to a range of libraries with different levels of business.

Table 9.1 Workloads generated by a modular staffing formula

Library workload (FTE)	Site A	Site B	Site C	Site D	Site E	Site F
Counter work	4.68	0.58	1.26	2.48	0.44	0.94
Shelving	1.75	0.20	0.44	0.91	0.16	0.32
Shelf tidy	1.90	0.19	0.33	0.58	0.14	0.29
Enquiry/message work	2.70	0.26	0.46	1.41	0.19	0.36
Additions	0.06	0.01	0.02	0.03	0.01	0.01
Stock maintenance	0.38	0.08	0.10	0.15	0.07	0.10
Technical allowance	0.66	0.18	0.18	0.39	0.18	0.18
Professional support	0.74			0.92		
Administration	2.16	0.15	0.26	0.65	0.11	0.21
Supervision	0.98	0.11	0.20	0.48	0.09	0.15
Administrative and secretarial assistants	2.00					
Reader development	0.41	0.04	0.02	0.32	0.02	0.02
IT	1.50	0.26	0.38	0.68	0.15	0.30
Stock editing	0.64	0.07	0.07	0.21	0.07	0.07
Specialist tasks/other posts	8.74	0.23	0.34	1.27		
Total	29.29	2.36	4.06	10.47	1.63	2.96

As can be seen, the proportion of total time represented by counter duties varies considerably according to the range of activity undertaken at each site. At Library A, although loans are significantly higher than those at any of the other libraries and generate a workload equivalent to 4.68 full-time staff, this is a much lower percentage (15.98%) of the total staffing than at Library B, where loans generate a workload of only 0.58 full-time equivalent staff, but account for 24.58% of the total staffing.

Using experience from the four existing RFID installations in the county, it was calculated that at least 50% of transactions should be accounted for by self-service. On this basis, 50% of staff time required for counter duties would need to be retained, but the other 50% capacity became available for reuse in other ways. In the event, it was decided that 35% would be used for a combination of contributing to the cost of the technology and efficiency savings, while the remaining 15% would be retained and reinvested in staffing to enable the introduction of floor walking, extended opening hours, or other customer-focused benefits (see Figure 9.1).

There is also a built-in incentive, if one were needed, in this approach for staff to encourage the public to use self-service. Any level of self-service use above 50% automatically becomes available for reinvestment, providing more staff time to carry out other duties.

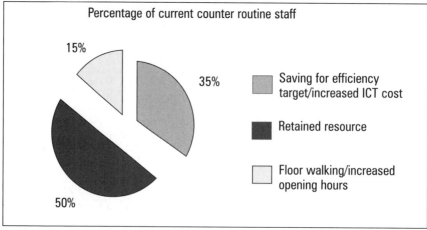

Figure 9.1   Use of saved staff time

Table 9.2 shows the effect of applying this to the existing staffing formula for each library.

Table 9.2 Savings attributable to RFID at individual libraries						
Workload (FTE)	Site A	Site B	Site C	Site D	Site E	Site F
Counter work	4.68	0.58	1.26	2.48	0.44	0.94
RFID counter work at 65%	3.04	0.38	0.82	1.61	0.29	0.61
Saving	1.64	0.20	0.44	0.87	0.15	0.33
Saving as % of total staffing	5.59	8.47	10.84	8.31	9.20	11.15

This approach confirms what might be assumed intuitively – that the largest savings are to be found at the busiest libraries, and that, because of the much wider range of activities that tend to occur at larger libraries, this saving will represent a smaller proportion of a large library's staffing than that for libraries where counter duties form the bulk of the staffing requirement.

However, it also demonstrates the advantage of having a formula to measure workload in some detail when dealing with smaller libraries, where the proportion of total staffing accounted for by counter duties can vary quite considerably.

Nevertheless, any limitations of the formula (how does staffing relate to opening hours, for example, rather than workload?) will then need to be taken into account.

The limitations of a formula-based approach go much beyond this, of course, and the implementation of any efficiency programme will have to reflect local and national policies, covering everything from union consultation to single staffing of service points, and ultimately redundancy if that is the path being followed. That being said, there seems to be remarkably little evidence of any extensive job losses resulting from the introduction of RFID, despite the emphasis on self-service. Staffing of establishments may certainly have been reduced, but where this is the case it has usually been achieved through natural wastage.

By far the most popular approaches seem to be redeployment, or the mix of savings and redeployment as described above. This may partly reflect

– in UK public libraries at least – the need to accommodate the extended range of roles that library staff have had to undertake since the introduction of the People's Network, the UK government's initiative to help public libraries provide universal access to the internet and information technology, without any increase in numbers (this type of work is also difficult to accommodate in staffing formulae of the kind described above). The more proactive role that RFID enables fits particularly well with the coaching and support tasks created as a result of this new service.

Summary

Used effectively, RFID saves staff time. These savings can be realized to make the library more efficient (using fewer staff) or more effective (using staff to provide value-added services), or a combination of the two. The use of staffing formulae can help make the calculation of the potential savings more accurate.

Chapter 10

Buying a system: evaluating the offers

How do you choose a system? How do you know it's the right one for you? How do you demonstrate it's the right one for you? How will it work with your LMS? How will your staff work with it?

Range of suppliers/range of responses

There is now a wide range of suppliers serving the library RFID market, and so any request for proposal (RFP) is likely to elicit a sizeable response. It will soon become clear that while some systems may be similar, there are big differences between others. The gradual establishment of standards is starting to reduce some of these differences by specifying approaches which will maximize interoperability and the most efficient ways of working, but they will nevertheless be put into practice in different ways by individual suppliers, while still conforming to the standard.

There is no single, perfect library RFID system that will meet everybody's needs, simply because everybody's needs are slightly (or sometimes, very) different. As a result, this range of responses should be seen as a good thing, and the sign of a healthy market. The challenge is to ensure that the most appropriate system is matched to the library concerned. It is also important to be able to demonstrate that this has been done.

Why systematic evaluation is important

Once the decision has been taken to adopt RFID, after determining the requirements and issuing an RFP from suppliers through the appropriate channels, a process will then be needed to ensure that the responses received from suppliers are evaluated in a systematic and fair way.

It perhaps should go without saying that this is an essential part of ensuring that the system chosen is the one which most closely meets the requirements that have been specified, but it is sometimes forgotten that, in addition, suppliers need to be confident that their responses are being considered against objective criteria that are applied consistently, rather than subjectively and randomly. Suppliers invest as much – if not much more – time in the process of responding to RFPs as their potential customers do, and expect that their efforts will be judged fairly.

How to evaluate systematically
Overview rating

Tables 10.1 to 10.7 show sample evaluation sheets, containing some of the higher-level elements that will almost certainly need to be considered as part of this process. This approach not only enables a score to be given to assess a system's performance of a particular operation, but also provides a total score that reflects the relative importance being given to that element through weighting. For example, it may be that a supplier offers excellent RFID library members' tickets, for which it would score highly, but that such a facility is not a high priority for this implementation, in which case its lower weighting would result in a lower total score.

Table 10.1 System's ability to realize the full range of benefits of RFID

Note: Scoring: 0 = Not available   1 = Poor   2 = Acceptable   3 = Good   4 = Excellent

Number	Description	Score	Weight	Total	Comments
1.1	Self-issue: able to deal with items a) In any plane? b) At an acceptable speed? c) Other				
1.2	Self-return: able to deal with items a) In any plane? b) In multiples? c) Other				
1.3	Stock taking a) Available? b) Accuracy? c) Other				
1.4	Security system a) Integrated? b) Add-on via separate system c) Other				
1.5	RFID/smart tickets a) Available/offered? b) Benefits? c) System works with third-party cards?				
1.6	Other				

Table 10.2 Ease of use (1): simplicity/complexity of processes

Number	Description	Score	Weight	Total	Comments
2.1	For staff				
2.1.1	Check-out/desensitizing: a) Number of movements b) Degree of difficulty c) Other				
2.1.2	Check-in/resensitizing a) Number of movements b) Degree of difficulty c) Other				
2.1.3	Stocktaking/inventory a) Number of movements b) Degree of difficulty c) Other				

Continued on next page

Table 10.2 *Continued*

Number	Description	Score	Weight	Total	Comments
2.2	For public				
2.2.1	Self-issue a) Number of steps b) Degree of difficulty c) Other				
2.2.2	Self-return a) Number of steps b) Degree of difficulty c) Other				
2.3	Other				

Table 10.3 Ease of use (2): equipment design/quality

Number	Description	Score	Weight	Total	Comments
3.1	Quality of design/usability/ergonomics				
3.2	Durability				
3.3	For stocktaking equipment specifically a) Portability b) Speed c) Accuracy d) Durability				
3.4	Other				

Table 10.4 Previous experience/levels of support offered

Number	Description	Score	Weight	Total	Comments
4.1	Number and size of libraries currently using system				
4.2	Feedback from existing sites?				
4.3	Level and availability of support – helpdesks etc.				
4.4	Value for money of warranty guarantee – coverage vs cost etc.				
4.5	Other				

Table 10.5 Stock security

Number	Description	Score	Weight	Total	Comments
5.1	Level of protection/loss rate – claimed Validated?				
5.2	Compatibility with other internal and external systems				
5.3	Level of false alarms				
5.4	Other				

Table 10.6 Conversion process

Number	Description	Score	Weight	Total	Comments
6.1	Ease of use of conversion equipment				
6.2	Number of tags that can be fitted per person hour Likely time required to convert 1000 items				
6.3	Availability of conversion equipment/numbers of units				
6.4	Cost of equipment purchase/hire?				

Table 10.7 Compliance with standards

Number	Description	Score	Weight	Total	Comments
7.1	ISO/IEC 18000 compliant? Fully?				
7.2	ISO 28560 compliant? Part 1 Part 2 Part 3 If not, is a transition plan available?				
7.3	Use of SIP2? Detailed exemplification?				
7.4	Other LMS interface used? Details?				

Rating of a specific element: how will it work with the LMS?

The relationship between the proposed RFID system and the LMS is of such crucial importance that it will usually justify an evaluation process specifically designed for the purpose. In this way, detailed aspects of the relationship can be assessed as well as an overview of the outcome. Tables 10.8 to 10.12 describe some of the main elements that will need to be rated.

Table 10.8 Tag/barcode compatibility

	Score	Weight	Total	Comments
Tags must be able to incorporate existing barcode numbers				
Tags can incorporate other data (can include part numbers, ISIL, supply chain status, etc.)				
Tags can be reprogrammed if barcodes are replaced				
Multiple items can be processed through existing LMS check-in/check-out screens				
No additional information needs to be stored on LMS for item identification				

Table 10.9 Staff hardware

	Score	Weight	Total	Comments
Readers can be switched between check-in and check-out functions as required				
Staff units can be deployed using existing furniture				
Staff units can interface with existing LMS PCs				
Staff units can be deployed using minimum power and network cabling				
Existing scanners/keyboards/mice can be still used on staff units				
Attachment of RFID readers to staff PCs will not affect existing software applications				

Table 10.10 Self-issue

	Score	Weight	Total	Comments
Self-check-out functionality is compatible with existing LMS system, including logging of charges				
RFID recognizes exception messages from LMS				
RFID can display appropriate exception messages to customer				
When exception message is displayed, no further items are desensitized				
If multiple items are being processed, progress should be clearly reported to customer on RFID screen				
RFID unit can accept payments by debit/credit and smart cards and update customer records on LMS accordingly				
RFID units can be placed within a reasonable distance of each other				
RFID units require minimal power and network cabling				
RFID units produce receipts detailing items issued and dates due back				
Wording of receipts is controllable by library staff				

Table 10.11 Self-return

	Score	Weight	Total	Comments
Self-check-in functionality is compatible with existing LMS system, including logging of charges				
If tag has been successfully read, an LMS exception message will not prevent it from being checked in or sensitized				
LMS exception messages can be viewed by staff as required				
LMS indicates to customer that item has been successfully checked in				
If multiple items are being processed, progress should be clearly reported to customer on RFID screen				

Continued on next page

Table 10.11 *Continued*

	Score	Weight	Total	Comments
RFID unit can accept payments by debit/credit and smart cards and update customer records on LMS accordingly				
RFID units can be placed within a reasonable distance of each other				
RFID units require minimal power and network cabling				
RFID units produce receipts detailing items issued and dates due back				
Wording of receipts is controllable by library staff				

Table 10.12 Technical problems

	Score	Weight	Total	Comments
RFID units will allow staff to check items in and out when LMS and or/network is unavailable				
If RFID uses an application controller, it allows staff to continue checking in and out when the controller is not available				
RFID units indicate to customer when LMS and or/network is unavailable on check-in and check-out units				

Overall assessment

Having considered each of these individual elements (and probably more), and the way in which the system interfaces with the LMS, it will then be necessary to come to an overall assessment. Table 10.13 offers an approach to arriving at an overall score: ideally, such a process will result in a maximum score of 100, but because of the amount of material that needs to be considered and the level of detail being reviewed, it is likely that – rather than resorting to scoring that involves fractions – reviewers will be more comfortable working with a larger range – as the 250 points total used here.

Table 10.13 Summary/overall scoring	
Feature	Score
Technology/compatibility with LMS • Tag/barcode compatibility • Staff hardware • Self-issue • Self-return • Technical problems	40 points

Self-service
• Flexibility of units
• Ease of use
• Check-in
  Income collection
  Staff intervention
  Receipts
  Out-of-hours use
  Request handling
  Non-book media
• Check-out
  Income collection
  Staff intervention
  Receipts (ability to turn off?)
  Out-of-hours use
• Non-book media
	40 points

Security
• Integrated
• Detection rate
  Books
  Non-book media
• De-activation
	30 points

Stock management
• Functioning hand-held device?
• Deals with
  Reservations?
  Stocktake/inventory?
  Circulating stock?
• Ease of use
• Speed
• Accuracy
	30 points

Staff use • Flexibility of units for check-in and check-out • Ease of use	20 points
Maintenance • Level of support • Out-of-hours provision • Cost	20 points

Continued on next page

Table 10.13 *Continued*	
Feature	Score
Training • On-site • Level of comprehensiveness	10 points

Conversion process
• De-activation of existing systems
  Ease
  Effectiveness
  Speed
• Tag application process
  Ease
  Accuracy
  Use with non-book media
  Need for additional equipment
	20 points

Supplier's ability to deliver • Experience in RFID • Reference sites • Company capacity • Company financial stability	20 points
Standards and interoperability • ISO 18000 • ISO 28560 • SIP	20 points
Total	250 points

Summary

Evaluating responses to an RFP is a crucial element in the process of adopting RFID. A systematic process needs to be followed. This will help ensure that the system chosen is the one that will most closely match the requirements of the library's business case, while adhering to relevant standards. It will also give suppliers confidence that their products are being considered fairly and consistently.

Chapter 11

Installing RFID: project management

> What needs to happen? In what order? Who's in charge?

Project management

Most library services will be part of a larger organization, whether a council, college or business, which will have its own approach to high-level project management, and to which the service will have to conform. This may be one of a variety of approaches, ranging from PRINCE2 to the simpler Critical Path Method, and a detailed description of this level of project management is outside the scope of this book. It is highly likely, however, that some form of Project Initiation Document (PID) will be required, describing in some detail why the project is required, how it will be managed, the costs and the planned outcomes.

In this way the parent organization can satisfy itself that its rules for capital investment will be met – and so make funds available – as well as minimize risk and ensure that the project is planned, organized and managed correctly. It will be crucial to the success of the project that the service meets all of its parent body's requirements in terms of project sponsorship, management and control, particularly if the release of funds is staged according to milestone targets being achieved.

Rather than dwelling on these vital but high-level and fairly generic aspects of project management, this chapter concentrates on the more pragmatic elements of putting library RFID into practice and outlines the main areas that will need to be covered.

Risk management

Regardless of the higher-level project management approach adopted, it is highly likely that some form of risk management process will be required. This can be comparatively straightforward, but needs to be an honest and robust assessment of the possible obstacles that might lie ahead and of the likelihood of their happening. Table 11.1 shows a simple chart, outlining some possible risks arising from RFID and assessing the level of their possible impact, with proposed plans to address them.

This approach is simple, but if used rigorously can still be effective. However, this rigour is vital if the process is not to be simply a token gesture. As Brealey and Myers (1991) point out in relation to corporate finance, a project is not a black box: 'A black box is something we accept and use but do not understand . . . we have been treating capital projects as black boxes [whereas] actual financial managers won't rest until they understand what makes the project tick and what could go wrong with it. Even if the project's risk is wholly diversifiable, you will still need to understand why the venture could fail.'

The main tasks
Tagging stock

This is likely to be the main determinant of the length of time the project will take: whether installing RFID in one library or fifty, it will not be possible for a library to go live until all its stock has been tagged. Tagging can be done using either the library's own staff, or an agency or, sometimes, the RFID supplier.

Use of an external organization may be neater, but is likely to be more expensive and the process less easy to control. It may also require the library's stock to be taken away from the building; this may be feasible in academic libraries, during the summer break for example. Mossop (2008), however, shows that this may not be necessary, making a convincing case for the contracting-out approach, with half a million items being successfully tagged and programmed in the space of five months (one month ahead of schedule) at the University of Central Lancashire.

Table 11.1 Risk assessment

Risk no.	Risk description	Probability	Impact	PI (probability x impact)	Mitigating strategy
1	Too many RFID initiatives being implemented within the same timescale	1	3	3	Establish realistic timeframes for each initiative
2	Too many other initiatives and the need to consider requirements from other groups	2	3	6	Review with library service management team
3	Arrangements for self-service payments delayed	2	3	6	Maintain dialogue with finance team
4	Building contractors unable to undertake work required on time	2	3	6	Establish realistic time frames
5	ICT contractors unable to undertake work required on time	2	3	6	Close project management of all contractors
6	Delay to the delivery of hardware	1	3	3	Firm delivery dates agreed
7	Insufficient library staff resources	2	3	6	Review with local managers
8	Unforeseen problems during implementation (health and safety etc.) beyond agreed closure period	1	3	3	Gather maximum amount of pre-project information
9	Library staff do not fully support RFID	1	3	3	Work closely with local staff to explain benefits
10	Library staff insufficiently trained	1	3	3	Implement training programme
11	Negative reaction from customers	1	3	3	Implement promotion plan
12	Tagging takes longer than planned	1	3	3	Implement contingency plan
13	Financial risk if implementation delayed beyond schedule	1	3	3	Continuous budget monitoring/liaison with finance

It seems to be less popular with public libraries, although where a service has its tags fitted and programmed by its book suppliers, any brand new library with entirely new stock will effectively have had its tagging outsourced.

The main advantage of using an external agency is usually seen as being the ability to specify a fixed completion date, avoiding all the concerns of managing what is essentially a very mechanical process, and so being able to concentrate on the more demanding elements of the project. However, some managers – regardless of the cost element – will nevertheless prefer to keep the entire process in-house, to be sure that everything is being kept on target.

The length of time required for the tagging process per library will depend on the number of tagging machines available and the level of staffing that can be devoted to the task, but crucially also the unit of time required to attach and to programme the tag for each item. This will vary considerably from system to system, depending on requirements – some taking less than a second to program the tag, others taking a little longer. However, the process of fitting and programming the tag itself is only one element – the other main aspect to be taken into account will be the length of time involved in handling the material. This will reflect the type of equipment available to the library – will the books need to be taken to a workroom, tagged and then returned to the shelves, or does the RFID supplier have portable tagging machines that can be taken to the material?

Some libraries have adopted one minute per item as a 'rule of thumb' guide to calculate the tagging time required for each library, covering all elements of the process. This is usually an overestimate (although some libraries, such as Santa Clara Public Library in California, have calculated it takes two minutes to complete the process) but it is nevertheless a useful guide. On this basis, a library with 20,000 stock items would need around 330 hours of staff time to complete its tagging: with two teams working full time with a tagging machine each, it should be possible to achieve this within five weeks or so.

For larger libraries, this will naturally be a bigger task, and if part of a larger programme of RFID installations they will need to be placed towards the end of the schedule to allow time for this. Table 11.2 shows a schedule for 16 libraries, mixing medium (20,000 stock – Library 1) with larger (40,000 stock – Library 5) and very large (250,000 stock – Library 15) across a period of ten months, with two sites going live each month.

Table 11.2 Tagging schedule

Month	1	2	3	4	5	6	7	8	9	10
Library										
1	Tag	Tag	Live							
2	Tag	Tag	Live							
3		Tag	Tag	Live						
4		Tag	Tag	Live						
5	Tag	Tag	Tag	Tag	Live					
6		Tag	Tag	Tag	Live					
7				Tag	Tag	Live				
8				Tag	Tag	Live				
9					Tag	Tag	Live			
10					Tag	Tag	Live			
11		Tag	Tag	Tag	Tag	Tag	Tag	Live		
12	Tag	Tag	Tag	Tag	Tag	Tag	Tag	Live		
13					Tag	Tag	Tag	Tag	Live	
14			Tag	Tag	Tag	Tag	Tag	Tag	Live	
15	Tag	Tag	Tag	Tag	Tag	Tag	Tag	Tag	Tag	Live
16							Tag	Tag	Tag	Live

Changes to the building and layout

As described in Chapter 7, the installation of RFID offers an opportunity to rethink the library's layout. Early consultation with local staff will be essential if the best results are going to be achieved. Apart from simply being good practice, the project may often provide the opportunity to correct long-standing problems in managing the building of which only local staff are aware, or to make improvements that take local circumstances into account which would otherwise not be possible. These early ideas will then need to be discussed with contractors and building management for a reality check, and to assess the likely cost.

In some cases, these discussions will result in plans for a very radical change, perhaps involving removal of walls or other significant building work, while in others changes may simply be the replacement and relocation of counters and enquiry desks. However, even in the latter case, it is likely that there will still need to be active management of the relationships between representatives of a number of separate organizations on site. These may include:

- the RFID supplier
- the LMS supplier
- the cabling contractor
- the telephony supplier
- the IT partner
- the flooring contractor
- the building and decorating contractor
- asset and facilities management.

Once plans have been finalized, it is useful to have a meeting where representatives of all of these parties are present to help to ensure that all the interdependencies have been taken into account, with work scheduled in the right sequence, and also to provide the opportunity for everybody involved to raise any problems or concerns. Table 11.3 provides an example of a checklist for such a meeting.

Table 11.3 Final meeting checklist		
Library:	Date:	
Communication and access	Responsibility	Information
Access to building • Keys • Alarms • Signing in		
Local contact		
Parking		
Emergency procedures		
Site clearance		
Furniture • Counter • Shelving/stock		
ICT equipment		

Table 11.3 *Continued*		
Library:	Date:	
RFID hardware	Quantity	
Self-service units • Self-issue • Self-return • Combined		
Desk • Low level • Standard		
Staff units		
Card readers		
Hand-held device		
Return chute		
Security gates		
Data/power requirements	Responsibility	
Clean power supply		
Cabling		
Gates		
Network requirements		
Patching		
Termination		
Telephony		
Location		
Flooring • Tiles • Carpet		
Decoration/other		
Asbestos register		
Induction loops		
Fire extinguishers		
Cleaning		
Lighting		
Schedule		
Closure date		

Continued on next page

Table 11.3 *Continued*		
Library:	Date:	
Schedule	Responsibility	Information
Contractors on site		
Reopening date		
Permissions		
Listed building?		
Landlord?		
Signage		

RFID hardware installation

Although this is the process at the heart of any RFID project, it is also usually the easiest and quickest element, as most library RFID units are almost 'plug and play' these days. However, for this to happen smoothly on the day, there needs to be close liaison between the RFID supplier's engineers and the other organizations involved – particularly building contractors and the LMS supplier. There also needs to have been prior agreement about the location of the self-service units in relation to the relocated counter and any security gates, and precise measurement of the distances between them to ensure no interference occurs between the different items of equipment.

Staff training

In terms of dealing with RFID equipment, there is usually remarkably little that staff need to be trained in, as most processes and procedures should be reasonably intuitive if the system has been designed correctly. It is likely that rather more time will need to be devoted to supporting staff in their new roles: this may include a new induction process and, if access to existing live sites is possible, visits to see RFID in action.

Promotion and publicity

The level, tone and detail of promotional material will need to be carefully judged and will vary according to local circumstances. Customers will need to be reassured that the system is easy to use, and that it represents an improvement to the service, but they will also want to know how it will benefit them in particular. In the UK Norfolk County Council, as part of its roll-out of RFID to libraries beyond its central library, made a specific point of engaging with the public through the use of focus groups to help ensure that the choice of system reflected the needs of its customers.

Notice of any library closures needed to install RFID will provide an early opportunity to explain what will be involved, and the planned outcomes. Once the system is live, bookmarks and posters may be useful to get across the main messages, but the system should usually be self-explanatory and not require detailed instructions.

The first day live

The key to a successful reopening following the installation of RFID – apart from the confidence that everything is working satisfactorily – is having enough staff on hand to be able to support customers, whether they are wanting to make use of the new system or, in the case of a substantial rearrangement of the building, need advice on the new location of their favourite material.

Experience in most RFID self-service libraries suggests that continued and sustained use of self-service later on is heavily dependent on the easy availability at this early stage of well-informed and helpful staff, able to demonstrate how to use the equipment and advise on any changes to procedures, such as the use of receipts instead of date labels.

Review and follow-up

Assuming that no emergency action is required following reopening, a review after the first month or so will be needed to confirm that the original decisions made when planning the installations were correct. Some adjustments will be easier to make than others – fine-tuning of the staffing levels is relatively easy to accommodate, whereas relocating the self-service units is likely to be rather more disruptive.

In the longer term, monitoring the take-up of self-service is likely to figure prominently in most managers' assessment of the success of a project. Such monitoring will also highlight any problem areas – if a library's performance is significantly lower than that of its peers, then this will usually warrant further investigation.

Ultimately, however, the key determinant of the success or otherwise of the move to RFID will be customer feedback and levels of use.

Summary

RFID installation is usually a major undertaking for a library. It will require effective project management of all aspects, from the comparatively theoretical approach of risk management to very pragmatic elements such as tagging stock and liaison with contractors. Staff training and promotion of the changes to the public will also need to be carefully planned, and evaluation of the project's success will need to reflect the business plan's objectives.

Chapter 12

Making the most of RFID: a case study

This chapter presents an example of a long-running RFID-based programme, designed to modernize a large public library service in the UK.

In the beginning . . .

When the library service of Essex County Council in the UK first became interested in RFID in the mid 1990s, it was for a very pragmatic reason. One of its largest libraries – Colchester, in the north-east of the county – had a radio frequency (RF) by-pass security system that had been installed in 1982. Such systems commonly work on one of two frequencies – 10.5 MHz and 8.2MHz – and at the time of the installation at Colchester, there were no regulations about which one should be used by libraries. Consequently, the 8.2 MHz frequency was chosen, as this was different from the 10.5 MHz used by the University of Essex (located nearby) so as to avoid causing problems for users of the two libraries. As the 'by-pass' element of the name suggests, the tags used in these systems remain permanently live and so taking a tagged item into an environment where the same frequency is used causes it to trigger the system's alarm.

A few years later, however, a protocol was devised to regularize the use of these two frequencies, so as to enable differentiation between use in the library environment and in retail. Unfortunately for Essex, the frequency allocated for retail use was the 8.2 MHz used in Colchester library, and as a result many of its customers found themselves setting off security system alarms in shops, simply by having a library book with them.

This was clearly a major public relations problem, with library users understandably concerned (at the very least) about being subjected to embarrassing and unnecessary searches and interrogations by retail security staff who were simply doing their job. The fact that this situation was nobody's fault – least of all that of the library service – was of little comfort or use in responding to the many resulting complaints.

Searching for a solution

As a result, the service began to investigate possible solutions. The simplest of these was to retag all of its stock at the new and correct 10.5 MHz frequency. Unfortunately, this would have been very expensive – with a total stock of around 250,000 items, it was estimated at the time that it would cost around £50,000 in staff time alone to complete the process, let alone the cost of the tags. While this would have solved the otherwise intractable problem of innocent library customers triggering alarms in their favourite shops – admittedly a very desirable outcome – it was a very costly approach with no other added value.

Consequently, it was decided to explore other possible options which might make better use of the staff time involved in retagging. Unfortunately, none was found, and for a few years the problem remained unresolved. However, when the first major library RFID applications began to be talked about in the mid 1990s, it appeared that this new technology might offer a way forward. As a result, attempts were made to find funding to put it into effect. One potential source that was identified was the Home Office's 'Chipping of Goods Initiative' (www.chippingofgoods.org.uk), designed to demonstrate the business benefits of using RFID and its ability to combat property crime, although this bid was unsuccessful.

An opportunity eventually arose as a result of the library service's Best Value review, which identified that Essex provided a good library service, but one which was 'traditional' and with little scope to adapt to future challenges. One of the main problems it faced was that its buildings were 'completely full' of stock and equipment, and – with growing evidence gathered from customer feedback indicating that queues and time-consuming procedures made libraries difficult to use for many people – it had no capacity to respond to these challenges.

Library management produced an action plan to follow this up, and proposed that self-service should be introduced into the county's busiest libraries. However, the technology – in particular the security systems – in use in these libraries was not able to support such a move. At the larger libraries in particular – including Colchester – where by-pass systems were in use, the introduction of self-service was especially problematic. Although security system suppliers had been experimenting with by-pass self-service, the resulting equipment had tended to be less than user friendly and not very robust.

As a result, a recommendation was made to the council to introduce RFID at Colchester library as a pilot, both to test its appropriateness as a self-service technology (no UK public libraries were using it at the time – the first major public library implementation would not occur until the opening of the Millennium Library at The Forum in Norwich in November 2001) – and to provide a value-added solution to the RF frequency problem there.

Looking for a supplier

This was approved, and a tender was subsequently placed for an RFID system for Colchester library. In contrast to the library RFID market today, where it is possible (and essential) to be very specific about many elements of the system required, the tender document was very short and comparatively open. Instead of concentrating on specific inputs, suppliers were asked to describe how they would provide 'a system that makes best use of RFID technology in a public library context'.

There were no other criteria, apart from an instruction that the tags to be used in the system should conform (as far as this was possible at the time) to industry standards, and not be adjusted to limit their use in any proprietary way, so making it possible for them to be obtained from sources other than the system supplier.

The response to the tender was encouraging, but it soon became clear that none of the proposed systems seemed to offer quite what the service was looking for. In some cases, the system offered was a hybrid – using an electromagnetic (EM) security solution, for example. This not only required two tags (EM and RFID) to be fitted to each item, but also limited the benefits to be gained from the RFID element: because the EM tag still had to be presented to the scanner in a particular plane and could not be read seemingly simultaneously with other items, the resulting self-service offer had little to differentiate it from existing barcode-based systems.

Other systems, while not requiring two tags, were unsuited to the service's requirements in other ways. Often, this was to do with the proposed tag's lack of compliance with industry standards, but other sources of concern included the way in which the system interacted with the LMS, and the user friendliness or otherwise of the self-service equipment.

The evaluation process made it clear that no supplier could provide what the service was seeking. Instead, the decision was taken to appoint a preferred supplier (Intellident) and to work with the company to try and produce a system which more closely matched what the service required.

Some 15 months later, this work was completed. A number of changes were made in the process, including a move from single-function self-service units to a multipurpose unit capable of dealing with self-issue, self-return, renewals and account checking in a user-friendly way via a touch screen, and able to separate requested and other exceptional items.

While the work on the development of the RFID system was under way, the non-technological elements of the project were also moved forward in detail. These included the design and branding of the new layout of the library, and staff development, and it soon became clear that these aspects of the project were not simply a support for the introduction of RFID. In fact, the converse had become true, and the technology – while clearly still crucial – was now seen as a catalyst for a fundamental change to service delivery and not simply a solution to a specific security problem.

Branding, guiding and layout

Essex had attempted previously to provide its libraries with more of a retail feel. This was because feedback from customers had indicated that, while they recognized that libraries were not shops, they nevertheless still judged them by High Street standards of presentation. Above all, they did not want a 'municipal' atmosphere, preferring an ambience and decor that was bright, clean and easy to use. However, efforts in that area had met with only limited success.

So – rather than reusing existing branding and signage – it was recognized that this project offered an opportunity to rethink service presentation, with interior design companies being invited to submit proposals for the 'makeover' of Colchester library – or, at least, with the limited resources available, the transformation of the entrance to the library so as to maximize the impact of RFID self-service.

The successful offer, provided by the design company curious oranj of Glasgow, presented a combination of creative reallocation of space, graphics, and use of colour to emphasize the self-service area. It also built on the determination of the service to greatly reduce the presence of the counter, both in size and in location. No longer the focal point at the entrance, the new counter would be much smaller and to one side of the main routes into the body of the library. Building on this approach, the designers produced signage which moved away from formal terminology such as 'enquiries', 'book return' or 'book issue', replacing it simply with 'hello'.

The self-service units were centrally placed, with screens facing the public on entry to and exit from the building in the newly liberated space formerly occupied by the counter, and self-evidently the key destination in that area. To further emphasize this, the units were placed on brightly coloured (green and cream) flooring indicating the self-service 'zone'. However, no other guiding or support material (least of all 'self-service here') was provided – the units themselves, with their on-screen help and their location on coloured flooring, were designed to be sufficiently distinctive without the need for posters or other guiding in the longer term.

The rebranding of the area also included graphics using simple, relevant library terms – 'read', 'surf', 'learn' and so on – which were reproduced on signage in the usual way, but also on large voiles – both to create a greater impact and also to help declutter the area by disguising the location of trolleys and other functional and operational furniture.

Staff roles

Clearly, if self-service were to be successful to any large extent, it would have an impact on the roles undertaken by staff, since much of their work revolved around the transactions carried out at the counter. There was an expectation that this would liberate enough staff time to enable the introduction of floor walking, providing more proactive and higher-level support for the public. However, at this stage there was no firm data on which to base such a move – even a small variation in take-up from that envisaged could result in the whole idea becoming impracticable.

As a result, floor walking was introduced in an exploratory way – staff were briefed on the basic concepts, but it was recognized that workflows might not always make it possible to put them into practice.

In the event, following Colchester's reopening with RFID self-service in September 2003, it soon became clear that take-up by the public was consistently at a level which would support a new role for staff, and that the level of input required to the more traditional roles at the counter could be greatly reduced. Self-service very quickly accounted for over 50% of loan transactions; interestingly, with much of the early emphasis having been on self-issue, it soon became clear that self-return – a facility not generally available with most barcode-based self-service machines – was even more popular.

Not only that, but the difficulties experienced by customers with retail security alarms had become a thing of the past.

Next stages

The high-profile use of a large and busy library such as Colchester to pilot such a major change in service delivery would not normally have been a preferred course of action, but the problems outlined above relating to its security system meant that no other option had been available. However, the fact that RFID self-service had been shown to work successfully in such a busy environment suggested that it should be a comparatively low risk to extend its use to other libraries. Consequently, the following year, with one site due for refurbishment and two others due to move to new premises, opportunities soon became available to explore the use of RFID in libraries of different sizes, and in different environments.

Basildon – the central library for the new town built mainly in the 1950s and 1960s – serving a population of around 80,000 in the south of the county, and so one of Essex's major town sites, lending over 300,000 items per year and located in a building shared with the district council's headquarters, had become due for refurbishment. Thaxted, on the other hand – a much smaller town in the north-west of the county with a population a little over 2500 – was due to move to larger premises shared with the local adult community learning centre. Finally, Bishops Park was the location for a new, extended school in the north-east of Essex, designed to become the community hub of the area, and included a new public library as part of its brief.

Each of these three libraries provided an opportunity to explore how RFID self-service could be used in very different situations to produce different benefits. In Basildon the results were similar in many ways to those achieved at Colchester, but on a slightly smaller scale – the front entrance of the library was opened up completely, the counter reduced in size, and staff freed to help the public more directly. In Thaxted, with the Adult Community College in the same building, self-service provided the opportunity for students to use the library when it was closed to the public. At Bishops Park, self-service offered the chance to extend the library's opening hours – at 45 hours per week, far higher than those that Essex would normally provide to a comparatively small community – without needing to provide staffing for the whole period, as the premises were shared with the school.

The roll-out

The success of RFID in these further three libraries made it clear that it would be possible to develop a business case to extend its use across the county. While it would have been feasible – as demonstrated by Thaxted and Bishops Park – to include libraries of all sizes, the economic reality of the situation meant that some kind of return on investment had to be achieved to justify investment by the council.

The business case

However, the only potential source of such a return was staffing, and so at least part of the business case had to be predicated on a reduction in the level of staff at each of the libraries involved. This immediately ruled out libraries below a certain size, since there was no scope for reducing their staffing to any degree. Nevertheless, 30 libraries were identified as having a sufficiently large staffing establishment to realize a saving, and a case was developed on that basis. This approach also enabled the service to demonstrate that it could make its contribution to the council's Gershon efficiency savings in this way.

However, the business case was not solely about 'cashable' benefits. It also outlined the many other advantages that RFID could bring to the service, even though they might be 'non-cashable', at least initially. The first of these was simply that the new approach to service delivery was very popular with customers at a time when public libraries across the country appeared to be falling out of favour. User surveys dating back to the Best Value review, and more recently a consultation called 'speak Up' which had resulted in 35,000 responses from Essex residents, had all pointed to the need for libraries to be easier to use, with self-service figuring highly in the ways that this might be achieved.

The ease with which libraries could be placed in buildings that could be shared with other services, whether colleges, schools, clinics, post offices or other community staples, was also highlighted. In addition, the ability to 'stretch' staffing across longer opening hours was seen as a major benefit, particularly for a service which, while it met most of the Public Library Service Standards (PLSS) quite comfortably, was some way below the requirements PLSS 12's 128 scheduled hours per 1000 population, at only 108.

All of this fitted well with the council's four principal priorities, as stated in the administration's manifesto - improving service, enhancing reputation, community leadership and value for money - and so the final version of the business case brought all of these elements together into a single transformational campaign, called 'Making it Happen' (MiH).

'Making it Happen'

MiH's aims were very simple:

■   to make Essex libraries welcoming and friendly places to be

■ to ensure customers can access services quickly and efficiently

■ to give staff the time and space to help and assist customers

■ to provide customers with the services they want.

Its success was to be judged against key targets in the following areas:

■ visits – to achieve a stretching target of 6600 visits per 1000 head of population (to achieve PLSS 6)

■ customer satisfaction – to achieve significant improvements in satisfaction levels

■ range of services – to deliver increases of 3% annually (against a current baseline of 458 different services currently offered through libraries)

■ efficiency gains – self-service to be taken up by 50% of library users, to realize £54,000 worth of savings in the first year, and more in the subsequent two years.

All of this was underpinned by a vision statement describing what a library that had successfully undergone the MiH programme would deliver – and how:

An Essex RFID library will be:

■ Welcoming

■ Easy to use

■ Stimulating

■ Contemporary

With employees at all levels, including front line and senior management, working with customers in a proactive manner to ensure that every customer transaction with Essex Libraries is positive and delivered by employees who are clearly enjoying their work . . .

The achievement of such a vision would not be possible simply through the application of technology, but would also need a change to existing working practices and the creation of a new role for staff providing direct support to the public. A new job title – Customer Services Assistant – reflected the fundamental change of emphasis in the job profile, which required increased and improved interpersonal skills, focused on ensuring that the library user would always enjoy the best possible experience on each visit. This was in marked contrast to the original profile for a Library Assistant, which had been much more concerned with process – the issuing and discharging of books, handling money and so on.

Staff development

Supporting and enabling staff to undertake such a major change in role required a staff development package which addressed all of these factors, and it was decided to blend three separate elements to provide what was needed. It had become clear, for example, that existing customer care training could not provide a basis for such a radically different approach to service provision, and so some kind of transformational intervention device was required to enable staff to make such a change.

Many such devices exist, but the one chosen was FISH! (Yokoyama and Michelli, 2004), as developed at the Pike Place Fish Market in Seattle. FISH! seemed a particularly useful approach, as it offered a way of empowering staff to provide excellent customer service through the use of four very simple principles. While two of these are common to most customer care packages – 'make their day' and 'being there' – and a third – 'have fun' – comes dangerously close to banality, the combination of the three with the final element – 'choose your attitude' can provide a very powerful mechanism which is both easily understood and capable of being translated into tangible benefits.

Overlaying this approach to customer care philosophy, it was recognized that some specific skills and techniques were required by staff in this new role. One of the packages used to address this was an online course called Frontline, produced by Opening the Book (www.openingthebook.com) and designed to provide greater access to the tenets of reader-centred work, originally developed as part of the Branching Out programme (www.branching-out.net), a UK initiative funded by the National Lottery and managed by the Society of Chief Librarians. This offers, among many other things, a structured approach to working with the public to help meet and develop their reading needs, and advice on how to display stock in the most effective way. As such, it offered a very useful platform to enable staff to deal confidently with the challenges they were likely to face in their everyday work, as well as the customer care skills provided in a library-specific context.

Finally, and linking with both FISH! and Frontline to complete the staff development package, it was decided to engage the services of a retail consultant who could apply the concepts used in commercial environments to a library environment. John Stanley Associates (JSA) (www.johnstanley.cc) is an Australian-based company with experience of this, which was appointed to help synthesize all of these different elements into a single transformational package.

Adding retail concepts

JSA's approach brings together retail techniques and philosophies regarding building layout and ambience - such as the 'hunters and gatherers' concept identified by Tim Denison at the University of Exeter in a report for Barclaycard, and Paco Underhill's work (Underhill, 2004), which identifies the importance of well-spaced aisles, and the use of 'decompression' or 'transition' zones to destress the customer - and applies them to the library context.

For example, Denison's findings as reported in the *Independent* (Frith, 2003) suggest that shoppers can be divided into 'hunters' and 'gatherers', the former having a clear idea of what they want and wishing to track it down immediately, and the latter having a less exact picture of what they want, wishing to take their time in finding it. According to Denison, most men (70%) are likely to be hunters, while most women (80%) tend to be gatherers, although these preferences may well differ according to circumstance. It is not too difficult to see a parallel between these roles and the library world's more usual terminology of 'searchers' and 'browsers', the first tending to make more use of the catalogue and not requiring staff help, while browsers are more likely to require staff assistance. The ability to recognize and differentiate between these two types is understandably of great value to any member of staff undertaking the floor-walking role.

Similarly, Paco Underhill's concept of the 'transition zone' in the retail world shows that shop and library staff alike seem to have generally been unaware of the need for a space in which customers can find their bearings and acclimatize to their surroundings when first entering a building. This need to 'destress' confounds the popular belief that important messages and prime material should be placed right at the entrance.

JSA uses workshops to explain these concepts and then helps staff build on them to produce standards for service presentation, ranging from cleanliness and tidiness of the library to staff's personal appearance, to help everybody involved to be clear about 'the way things are done around here'. In this way, the work is also transformed from a one-off exercise into an integral part of service management, ensuring that the practice is consistently applied across different sites and over time.

The customer experience

Underlying this use of staff development and retail techniques, however, was an element that some critics of current UK public libraries say has been lost sight of, which is the promotion of books and reading. MiH was designed, as much as anything else, to improve the customer experience by making it easier to find books. The primacy of the book and reading had always central to Essex Libraries' service philosophy – as it is for most services – and the quality of its book stock had been recognized in 'excellent' ratings in the Audit Commission's Stock Quality Health Check, carried out from 2000 onwards. The service had also consistently increased the quantity of books it purchased from the mid 1990s on, buying 50% more books in 2004 than it had in 1992, and provided support to over 400 reading groups.

Despite this, however, there was evidence from user surveys that customers were not always able to find the material they were looking for, and so MiH looked for ways to improve this situation. The most direct way of doing this was to introduce 'Express Zones' close to the entrance of each library, offering face-on display for books that 'you don't have to think twice about borrowing'. This strap-line provided staff with a simple aide-memoire regarding the kind of stock that should be promoted in this way, avoiding the need to add 'Express Zone' stickers to books while also ensuring that the content of the Express Zones remained dynamic, rather than being limited to specific titles or genres.

The outcome
Delivery

One of the initial challenges of a programme such as MiH – involving RFID, building works, rebranding, staff development and marketing and promotion to the public – is simply to deliver it as planned. Thirty-one libraries were eventually included in the MiH programme, which began in January 2006 and was completed in March 2007, on schedule and within budget.

One interesting change that had occurred during the period between the first four libraries going live and the development of the business case for the extension to the further 31 libraries was that Essex County Council had entered into a strategic partnership with BT for provision of its ICT service. This provided useful additional help in terms of support for project management and other areas, but also added a further level to the number of partners and contractors that needed to be managed and kept up to date with developments.

Take-up

With regard to the level of public take-up of self-service, the original business plan target of 50% of transactions was met very early on and consistently exceeded by all libraries, reaching 60.2% of loans and 76.3% of returns by November 2006. (At the time of writing, this has improved further, so that 37 live sites now achieve an average of 92% of returns and over 70% of loans.) As a result, more staff time has become available for reinvestment in the service, providing more opportunity for one-one-support and advice for borrowers.

The popularity of self-service also meant that the planned savings were able to be realized: with £54,000 being saved in 2006-7, reaching a total of £167,000 per annum from 2008–9 onwards, 21 posts were saved through natural wastage, thus achieving all of the required efficiencies, paying for the technology and making the required contribution to the Gershon agenda. In addition, over 50% of MiH libraries exceeded their visitor targets within the first year, with some doing so by a significant margin. This also resulted in increased loans – at the time of writing, some 18 months after the completion of this phase of MiH, the county's libraries are now showing positive growth in book issues for the first time since 2001.

Customer satisfaction

Accompanying this growth in use has been a significant rise in customer satisfaction. In the Best Value General Satisfaction survey in 2003, overall satisfaction with the library service for Essex residents stood at 72%. In the summer of 2006, the independent research firm BMG carried out a tracker survey in which the same question was put to the general public. This time, overall satisfaction was found to be 77.8%. This increase of 5.8 percentage points is statistically significant, and the bulk of the improvement came from more people saying they were 'very satisfied' rather than either 'fairly satisfied' or 'neither satisfied nor dissatisfied', as shown in Figure 12.1.

Regular library users also registered increased satisfaction with the service in the regular assessments carried out using CIPFA's PLUS surveys. In particular, the concern regarding readers' ability to find specific books

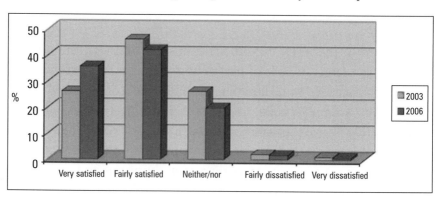

Figure 12.1   Changes in public satisfaction with Essex Libraries 2003–6

appeared to be starting to be addressed: ratings improved from 70% in 2005 to 75.9% in 2006.

The largest increase in customer satisfaction, however, was in the percentage of customers rating staff helpfulness as 'very good', as shown in Table 12.1.

Table 12.1 Staff helpfulness ratings in CIPFA Plus survey

	Staff helpfulness				
	Very good	Good	Adequate	Poor	Very poor
2003	66.6%	30.5%	2.6%	0.3%	0.1%
2004	68.7%	28.6%	2.4%	0.3%	0.0%
2006	81.8%	16.6%	1.4%	0.1%	0.1%

Although it is not possible to ascribe a causal link between all of these improvements in user perception and increased uptake with the MiH programme, it is at the very least encouraging that the areas of improvement have been those on which the programme focused. In particular, the effect of FISH! on customers' perception of staff helpfulness seems to have been especially acute, with the emphasis on the importance of attitude perhaps being the crucial element that made the difference when compared to previous approaches to customer care training.

The future

In light of this success, it is probably not surprising that the service should look to a further phase of MiH, and extend it to all of its 73 libraries. At the time of writing, a business case for this has been approved, aimed at installing RFID self-service and stock management into all 33 remaining libraries over a 12-month period. This business case, however, is different from that for the previous roll-out in one particular respect. Its main aims remain the modernization of the service at these sites, improvement of the customer experience, and more flexible use of the buildings to enable partnership working and delivery of a wider range of council services. However, it recognizes that, with smaller libraries being involved, there is no scope for staff savings in this process.

Nevertheless, it is still possible to demonstrate how the extension of RFID can reduce the council's costs when used in combination with another technology. The programme is scheduled to coincide with the installation of a free Wi-Fi service to all Essex libraries. Clearly, this will further improve the service to the public and will also mean that building layouts can be even more flexible, with fewer fixed points determined by cabling and other requirements. It will also mean that – in addition to the improved service being provided to the public – libraries can act as 'touch-down' centres for peripatetic employees of the wider council and its partner organizations, enabling savings to be made through the closure of expensive satellite offices.

Separately from this, planning is also under way to use RFID in the acquisitions process, to speed up the receipting of the half a million or so new items added to stock by the county each year.

How important is RFID to this case study?

Although RFID is at the heart of all that was carried out in these projects, it has already been noted that it was really a catalyst for a much wider programme of activity rather than an end in itself. One key question arising from this is whether the programme could have been achieved without RFID, through the use of some other enabling device.

The answer to this is that it probably could have been, as many of the ingredients of 'Making it Happen' – the use of retail techniques, branding, staff training – are things which are not dependent on any form of technology. However, it is likely that either the level of success would have been much lower, or some other kind of investment would have been necessary. It is possible that barcode-based self-service may have freed staff from routine counter work, but the limited experience that Essex had in this area indicated that it would have been much more difficult to achieve the same level of take-up by the public. The increased flexibility of the buildings resulting from the introduction of self-service may also have been achievable in other ways, but it is difficult to see what they may have been.

Summary

Overall, RFID has proved to be the key to modernizing the service in Essex in a way that was both affordable and easily implemented. Essex, in common with many other library services in different sectors, has been able to demonstrate that RFID provides a platform for improving both customer satisfaction and use while still making financial savings, and so achieving the targets of increasing both efficiency and effectiveness.

Chapter 13

RFID, libraries and the future

The use of RFID in libraries has grown rapidly since the late 1990s, and has become a fundamental element in the design of many new major libraries around the world – from Seattle in the USA to Shenzhen in China. In some of these large libraries – Shenzhen has a stock of 2 million items, Seattle has capacity for nearly 1.5 million – this has included not only self-service but also automated stock handling. At Seattle, between 1100 and 1400 items can be dealt with per hour, returning them to the correct part of the library's 'book spiral', spread over four storeys.

However, the primary focus of most current implementations remains self-service, with the supply chain applications commonly found in other industries being adopted only in those countries where a centralized process is already in place. While frustrating to some observers, anxious to see the full benefits of RFID being exploited by libraries, it is perhaps understandable that library managers have concentrated on the 'quick win' that self-service provides. It is also possible to argue that, to some extent, libraries' use of only a limited element of this technology's potential is no different from that of software generally.

According to the widely quoted statistics researched by the Standish Group (Johnson, 2002), only 20% of the features in enterprise software are ever used, with 19% rarely used and 45% never used. This may be partly a reflection of the trend towards software 'bloat', but also aligns with the familiar findings of Pareto's principle, with 80% of effects attributable to only 20% of causes.

More importantly, there are some aspects of RFID that, once taken for granted, are now being questioned. A statistic often quoted in the early days of library RFID was that tags would be able to achieve at least 100,000 cycles (or 50,000 loan and 50,000 return transactions) and so would easily outlast the items to which they were attached. More recently, however, 3M has suggested that not all tags are created equal, with some becoming inactive within a very short time, due to environmental effects (mainly heat) or simply the use of lower quality materials in construction (3M Library Systems, 2007).

Some libraries have experienced similar effects, but due to a different cause – some tags may go into 'sleep mode', a feature designed mainly for the retail trade to help make them more secure in certain circumstances. This can be remedied, but until then it makes such tags completely dysfunctional in a library setting.

Such practical problems are perhaps to be expected when using a comparatively new technology in a new situation, however, and are generally resolved without too much difficulty, albeit at some expense

New and developing uses for RFID

Meanwhile, other, more imaginative uses of RFID are also starting to appear. The audioindex project at the public library of the Umea region in Sweden is one example of how RFID's capability to interact with other technologies can be exploited to produce something new and different. However, there are now other projects which go beyond the purely transactional and begin to explore the ways in which RFID can help to make the hybrid library concept much more of a reality. RFID is a key element in parts of the Thinkering Spaces project (www.id.iit.edu/ThinkeringSpaces) at the Illinois Institute of Technology's Institute of Design in Chicago, providing a 'mashed-up library' where children can experience books alongside other technologies in a completely new way, and where the learning experience in a library is fundamentally altered. The website states that the project's objectives are to:

■ Envision a *third* place in libraries that engages kids in hands-on, heads-on, physical/virtual interplay and collaboration.

■ Describe a modular and adaptive structural system that is independent of building architecture and supports various exploratory activities.

■ Frame an open source interface management system that is compatible with off-the-shelf technologies and allows developers to create new applications.

■ Enable content to be derived from existing library programs, initiated by national organizations, developed by individual librarians or created by kids themselves.

It is also possible that new hardware may be the source of a different kind of library RFID application in the future. One current example of how the concept of self-service might be extended further can be found at Shenzhen library (Xinhuanet, 2008), which has piloted a self-contained 'automated library machine'. This is similar in concept to a bank's cash machine, but allows the loan and return of books. It means that mini-branches can be located in non-library locations such as supermarkets and railway stations, with the service available on a 24-hour basis. Although currently only capable of holding 400 books at any one time, the machine is linked to the service's LMS, and so is able to provide a request service in the same way as a regular branch. Notification of the availability of a requested item for collection is sent by text message, with the book being delivered to the machine closest to the requestor. Although some further development is still required before the machine can be used in a wider range of locations (it can currently only be used indoors, although this is being worked on), Shenzhen plans between 30 and 50 installations around the city during 2008, at a cost roughly equivalent to $57,000 per machine.

Other new functionality is also likely to be of significant interest to library managers. Some of this may revolve around Near Field Communication, and the facility within mobile phones to function as scanners to enable remote renewal, or as electronic purses for payment of charges – this is already available in some car parking operations.

Developing tag technology

Perhaps the area where further development will provide the most benefit and challenge from a library point of view, however, is that of tags. The imminent introduction of ISO/IEC 18000-3 Mode 3 tags, mentioned in Chapter 4, offers the possibility of exciting new functionality and performance. In the longer term, it is possible that development of lower-cost, printed-electronics RFID tags may at some point provide a way for publishers to incorporate tags into books as part of routine production. Such a possibility is very enticing, and offers the prospect of a far more efficient supply chain for libraries – especially those in countries where the distribution of books to libraries is at best decentralized and at worst Byzantine.

Nevertheless, despite the rapid growth predicted for printed electronics, particularly in the period up to 2012, it seems unlikely that the technology will develop sufficiently to enable the kind of use that libraries would want to make of it during that period. Although printed electronics can produce tags much more cheaply than current methods, at the time of writing the resulting product has a much more limited read range – up to a maximum of 50cm. This may well improve in future, but – as with the current generation of RFID – this will depend on the establishment of standards and the other supporting infrastructure that is required for successful interoperability.

Conclusion

Perhaps the most realistic (if not hopeful) assessment is that RFID will simply become as much a routine and integral part of library technology as the barcode is today. Most of the building blocks for this to happen are now starting to be put into place, particularly as ISO 18000 and ISO 28560 have begun to provide a way forward for interoperability of systems and tags, enabling the introduction of further standardization across other aspects of RFID. Building on this, perhaps some time in the future an LMS will be developed that fully incorporates RFID as an integral part of its technology, rather than requiring an interface between two separate systems.

Meanwhile, any doubts over privacy need to be resolved, Although there has been remarkably little concern about this in Europe, it may yet become the focus of media attention in the future, at which point, as the largest users of item-level tags, libraries would have to be very clear about the precautions and protections that they had in place to prevent any abuse of the personal data they held.

Regardless of these potential future developments, and of existing problems, the rate of growth in the use of RFID by libraries around the world continues to increase rapidly, to the extent that – while still clearly developing and adapting to the demands made of it – it is no longer seen as a novelty, but much more as a significant tool that enables library managers to transform and modernize their services in a way that meets the needs of their 21st-century customers.

Further information

Websites

BIC

www.bic.org.uk

> Book Industry Communication promotes supply chain efficiency through the use of standards, and this site has links to the E4Libraries project, including case studies and presentations, as well as details of the BIC/CILIP RFID in Libraries Working Group.

ISO 28560

http://biblstandard.dk/rfid/publicdocsbefore.htm

> This site, hosted by the Danish Agency for Libraries and Media, contains all details of the meetings and publications of Working Group 11, the group responsible for the development of ISO 28560.

NISO

www.niso.org/apps/group_public/workgroup.php?wg_abbrev=rfid

> This site, home of the USA's NISO group for library RFID, includes details of its meetings, and various documents, including recommendations for best practice and responses to the draft ISO 28560 standard.

Forums
LIB-RFID-UK

www.jiscmail.ac.uk/cgi-bin/webadmin?A1=ind0812&L=LIB-RFID-UK
> A valuable source of information, advice and polemic about library RFID in the UK.

RFID-LIB

http://listsmart.osl.state.or.us/mailman/listinfo/rfid_lib
> A discussion list for library RFID, hosted by Oregon State Library, this forum performs a similar function for the USA and includes much of interest to the European reader as well.

Blogs

A number of general library blogs refer to RFID from time to time – including Tim Coates's Good Library Blog (www.goodlibraryguide.com/blog) – but there are very few entirely devoted to the topic. One exception is the blog linked to the CILIP RFID in Libraries annual conference: http://communities.cilip.org.uk/blogs/rfid/default.aspx.

Library RFID system suppliers

There are now many of these worldwide. The following is a list mainly of those working in the UK, although some other major companies are also included.

2CQR
> 2CQR House
> Unit 2
> Long Bennington Business Park
> Main Street
> Long Bennington
> Lincolnshire NG23 5JR
> 0845 882 2778
> www.2cqr.com

3M Library Services

3M Centre
Bracknell
Berkshire RG12 8HT
0800 389 6686
http://solutions.3m.co.uk/wps/portal/3M/en_GB/LibrarySys/Home

Bibliotheca RFID Library Systems

Hinterbergstrasse 17
6330 Cham
Switzerland
+41 41 7269955
www.bibliothecarfid.com

Booktec Information Co

6F, 230 Bade Road
Section 3
Taipei
Taiwan
+886 2 25778838
www.rfid-library.com

Checkpoint Systems

101 Wolf Drive
Thorofare NJ 08086
USA
+1 800 2575540
www.checkpointsystems.com
(NB - although still very active in RFID generally, Checkpoint now sells
its library systems through 3M)

Civica (UK)

Plane Tree Crescent
Feltham
Middlesex TW13 7DT

020 8844 2121
www.civicaplc.com/uk

D-Tech International (distributors of Bibliotheca in the UK)
Building 136 Bentwaters Parks
Rendlesham
Woodbridge
Suffolk IP12 2TW
01394 420077
www.d-techdirect.com

DS
Hall View Drive
Bilborough
Nottingham NG8 4GD
0115 900 8000
www.ds.co.uk

Envisionware
2819 Premiere Parkway NW
Suite 350
Duluth GA 30097-8917
USA
+1 800 2168370 (020 7101 9619 within the UK)
www.envisionware.com

Intellident
Intellident House
Southgate 3
323 Wilmslow Road
Stockport SK8 3PW
0161 498 1140
www.intellident.co.uk

Intrepid Security

Unit 1 Mill Farm Business Park
Millfield Road
Hounslow
Middlesex TW4 5PY
020 8893 9922
www.intrepidsecurity.com

Libramation Library Services

12527 129 Street NW
Edmonton AB
Canada
+1 780 4435822
www.libramation.com

Nedap (Great Britain)

1 Hercules House
Calleva Park
Aldermaston
Berkshire RG7 8DN
01189 821038
www.nedaplibrary.com

Plescon Security Products

Unit 9 Sterling Complex
Sproughton Business Park
Farthing Road
Ipswich IP1 5AP
01473 745375
www.plescon.co.uk

SB Electronic Systems (distributors of Codeco in the UK)

Arden Grove
Harpenden
Hertfordshire AL5 4SL

01582 769991
www.telepen-barcode.co.uk

ST Logitrack Pte

Blk 1003 Bukit Merah Central
3-10 Redhill Industrial Estate
Singapore 159836
+65 6277 2882
www.stlogitrack.com

Tagsys (Europe)

180 Chemin de St Lambert
13821 La Penne sur Huveaune
France
+33 491275700
www.tagsysrfid.com

VTLS

1701 Krafts Drive
Blacksburg VA 24060
USA
+1 800 4688857
www.vtls.com

References

3M Library Systems (2006) *3M Standard Interchange Protocol*,
    http://multimedia.mmm.com/mws/mediawebserver.
    dyn?6666660Zjcf6lVs6EVs66S0LeCOrrrrQ-.

3M Library Systems (2007) *RFID 401: tag quality and reliability*, White
    Paper.

Albrecht, K. and McIntyre, L. (2006a) *Spychips: how major corporations
    and government plan to track your every move with RFID*, Nelson
    Current, 2006.

Albrecht, K. and McIntyre, L. (2006b) *The Spychips Threat: why Christians
    should resist RFID and electronic surveillance*, Nelson Current, 2006.

Batista, E. (2003a) *Chilly forecast for smart fridge*,
    www.wired.com/science/discoveries/news/2003/08/59858.

Batista, E. (2003b) *Step back for wireless IDtech?*
    www.wired.com/gadgets/wireless/news/2003/04/58385.

Bender, K. (2006) Berkeley Library Rift reaches Resolution, *Oakland
    Tribune*, (9 June).

Blacktown City Council (2008) Press release: *Blacktown City Libraries
    Lead Through Technology*, 11 July,
    www.blacktown.nsw.gov.au/news-and-events/news-releases/
    blacktown-city-libraries-lead-through-technology.cfm.

Bloomfield, S. (2006) How an Oyster Card could Ruin Your Marriage, *The Independent*, (19 February).

Book Industry Study Group (2004) *BISG Policy Statement POL-002*, BISG.

Boss, R. (2001) *RFID Technology*, http://archive.pla.org/publications/technotes/technotes_rfid.html.

Brealey, R. and Myers, S. (1991) *Principles of Corporate Finance*, 4th edn, McGraw-Hill.

Cardullo, M. (n.d.) *Genesis of the Versatile RFID Tag*, www.rfidjournal.com/article/view/392/1/2.

Cavoukian, A. (2004) *Guidelines for Using RFID Tags in Ontario Public Libraries*, www.ipc.on.ca/images/Resources/rfid-lib.pdf.

Chacra, V. and McPherson, D. (2003) *Personal Privacy and Use of RFID Technology in Libraries*, VTLS.

Checkpoint (2000) Press release: *Checkpoint Systems Beat Competition*, 10 July, www.meto.com/download.aspx?page=librarysuccessstories.

Christensen, C. (1997) *The Innovator's Dilemma: when new technologies cause great firms to fail*, Harvard Business School Press.

Collins, J. (2004) *Marks and Spencer Expands RFID Trial*, www.rfidjournal.com/article/articleview/791/1/1/.

Commission of the European Communities (2007) *Results of the Public Consultation on Future RFID Technology Policy*, http://ec.europa.eu/information_society/policy/rfid/doc/rfidswp_en.pdf.

Curran, K. and Porter, M. (2007) A Primer in Radio Frequency Identification for Libraries, *Library Hi Tech*, **25** (4), 595–611.

DCMS (Department of Culture Media and Sport) (2000) *DCMS/Wolfson Public Library Challenge Fund Annual Report 1999/2000*.

DCMS (Department of Culture Media and Sport) (2003) *Framework for the Future*.

EFF (Electronic Frontier Foundation) (2004) *Action Alert: a chance to keep RFIDs out of San Francisco public libraries*, http://w2.eff.org/Privacy/Surveillance/RFID/sflibrary.

European Commission (2005) *Working Document on Data Protection Issues Related to RFID Technology*, http://ec.europa.eu/justice_home/fsj/privacy/docs/wpdocs/ 2005/wp105_en.pdf.

Frith, M. (2003) How Couples Can Shop Till They Drop – for 72 Minutes, *The Independent* (17 September).

Global RFID Interoperability Forum for Standards (2008) *RFID Standardisation State of the Art Report*, www.grifs-project.eu/data/File/GRIFS%20D1_3%20State%20of %20the%20Art%20Report.pdf.

HSE (Health and Safety Executive) (UK) (2007) *Applications of RFID Technology, HSE Horizon Scanning Intelligence Group Short Report SRO11*.

ICNIRP (International Commission on Non-Ionizing Radiation) (2004) ICNIRP Statement Related to the Use of Security and Similar Devices Utilizing Electromagnetic Fields, *Health Physics*, **87** (2), (August), 187–96, www.icnirp.org/documents/EASD.pdf.

Institute of Electrical and Electronics Engineers (1991) *IEEE Standards Association: Standard for Safety Levels with Respect to Human Exposure to Radio Frequency Electromagnetic Fields, 3 kHz to 300 GHz*, http://standards.ieee.org/reading/ieee/std_public/description/ emc/C95.1-1991_desc.html.

JISC (Joint Information Systems Committee) (2006) *Designing Spaces for Effective Learning: a guide to 21st century learning space design*, HEFC.

Johnson, J. (2002) *Keynote speech at XP 2002*, www.xp2003.org/xp2002/talksinfo/Johnson.pdf.

Kharif, O. (2006) What's Lurking in that RFID Tag?, *Business Week*, (16 March).

Kravets, D. (2008) *Farmers see 'Mark of the Beast' in RFID Livestock Tags*, http://blog.wired.com/27bstroke6/2008/09/farmers-decryin. html.

LAMSAC (Local Authorities Management Services and Computer

Committee) (1976) *The Staffing of Public Libraries*, DES, 1976.

Lichtenberg, J. (2004) *RFID: coming to a library near you*, quoted in http://siliconinvestor.advfn.com/readmsg.aspx?msgid=20656501.

Lindl, B. (2005) Libraries Embrace Wireless, *UPI Wireless World*, (21 October).

Livingston, K. and Tam, J. (n.d.) *Authentication and Encryption of RFID Tags*, www.cs.stevens.edu/~klivings/Encrypting%20RFID%20Tags.ppt.

McCue, A. (2003) *Privacy Groups Protest RFID Tagging of Razors*, http://news.zdnet.co.uk/emergingtech/0,1000000183,39115718,00. htm.

McCue, A. (2006) *Football Club Tags Fans with RFID Tickets*, www.silicon.com/retailandleisure/0,3800011842,39163900,00. htm.

Miller, V. (2008) Oyster Card: fears over Mifare security, *Daily Telegraph*, (21 June).

Moen, N. (2006) *Places and Spaces: public libraries for the 21st century*, Christchurch City Libraries, 2006.

Molnar, D. and Wagner, D. (2004) Privacy and Security in Library RFID: issues, practices and architectures, www.eff.org/Privacy/Surveillance/RFID/molnar_paper.pdf.

Morton, S. (2004) Barcelona Clubbers Get Chipped, BBC News, (29 September), http://news.bbc.co.uk/1/hi/technology/3697940.stm.

Mossop, S. (2008) *RFID at the University of Central Lancashire: a case study*, University of Central Lancashire.

Muir, S. (2007) RFID Security Concerns, *Library Hi Tech*, **25** (1), 95-107.

Oldenberg, R. (1989) *The Great Good Place*, Paragon House.

Randall, N. (2006) New York Notes, *Publishing News*, (14 October).

RFID Gazette (2006) *RFID Applications for Libraries*, (5 July), www.rfidgazette.org/2006/07/rfid_applicatio.html.

Smart, L. (2004) Making Sense of RFID, *Library Journal (Netconnect)*, www.libraryjournal.com/article/CA456770.html.

Snelling, C. (2005) Self Issue: not a quick win, *CILIP Update*, (April).

Sterling, B. (1994) *The Hacker Crackdown*,
www.chriswaltrip.com/sterling/crack0p1.html.

Strassman, P. (1996) *The Value of Computers, Information and Knowledge*, (30 January),
www.strassmann.com/pubs/cik/cik-value.shtml.

Thompson, G. (1989) *Planning and Design of Library Buildings*, 3rd edn, Butterworth Architecture.

Umea (2007) *Project Bibliotek 2007*,
www.umea.se/download/18.7f72e05d10d356aab3480004935/presentation_riga.pdf.

Underhill, P. (2004) *Why We Buy: the science of shopping*, Touchstone.

Urban Libraries Council (2006) *The Engaged Library: Chicago stories of community building*,
www.urbanlibraries.org/files/ULC_PFSC_Engaged_0206.pdf.

Ward, M. (2006) *Viruses Leap to Smart Radio Tags*,
http://news.bbc.co.uk/1/hi/technology/4810576.stm.

Woodward, J. (2007) *What Every Librarian Should Know about Electronic Privacy*, Libraries Unlimited.

Xinhuanet (2008) *Automated Library Machine Debuts in Shenzhen*,
www.xinhuanet.com/english/2008-04/08/content_7942201.htm.

Yokoyama, J. and Michelli, J. (2004) *When Fish Fly: lessons for creating a virtual and energized workplace from the world famous pike place fish market*, Hyperion.

Young, K. (2004) Inside IT: RFID tags and library books, *The Guardian*, (11 November).

Index

Web Accessibility
Practical advice for the library and information professional

Jenny Craven, editor

With ever greater provision of resources in electronic formats, formal recognition is increasingly being given to the growing awareness within the information profession that it is a moral duty as well as a legal requirement to take every feasible step to ensure that no one is excluded from access to goods and services, including web-based information and resources.

This timely book provides a practical introduction to web accessibility and usability specifically for information professionals, offering advice from a range of experts and experienced practitioners on the concerns relevant to library and information organizations. Contents include:

■ tools used for widening access to the web
■ Design for All – how web accessibility affects different people
■ the importance of web accessibility
■ accessibility advice and guidance
■ accessibility evaluation and assessment
■ issues for library and information services
■ Design for All in the library and information science curriculum
■ best practice examples of web accessibility
■ web accessibility in the future.

This approachable guide will enable information practitioners, web designers, trainers and students new to web accessibility to gain a good understanding of the issues involved in this vital area.

2008; 176pp; hardback; 978-1-85604-625-1 (accessible pdf version 978-1-85604-660-2); £44.95

Going Beyond Google
The invisible web in learning and teaching

Jane Devine and Francine Egger-Sider

Google isn't up to the task when it comes to serious research, and though your users and students have heard of the 'invisible', or 'deep' web, they probably have no idea how to tap into it. You need practical tools and strategies for teaching them about the web sources and specialized databases they will never find using everyday search engines.

This book will show you in simple, non-technical terms how to integrate the invisible web into teaching opportunities wherever they occur – in a one-on-one 'teaching moment' at the reference desk, or in a formal course. Estimated at 500 times the size of the visible web, the invisible web and the search skills needed to plumb its depths should be a part of every information literacy and research skills course. With this book you get expert teaching tips and scripts for informal instruction, plus model activities and assignments for the classroom. Key areas covered are:

- searching habits of students and other cohorts
- characteristics of the invisible web
- the visible versus the invisible web
- analysis of results from a model research assignment
- use of the invisible web at the reference desk
- use of the invisible web for library instruction
- use of the invisible web in Blackboard
- techniques for teaching the invisible web.

Statistics and summaries of relevant research will help you combat myths like 'Searching is easy', or 'Everything important is free'. Read this book too, to find out how the best deep web search tools, including CompletePlanet, Closer Look, and the Librarians' Internet Index, are evolving and what it all means for your library's future electronic collection development plans.

March 2009; 162pp; paperback; 978-1-85604-658-9; £44.95

Access, Delivery, Performance
The future of libraries without walls

Jillian R. Griffiths and Jenny Craven, editors

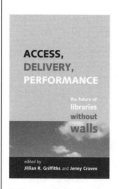

This book celebrates and acknowledges the contribution Professor Peter Brophy has made over a career spanning 37 years to the field of library and information studies. Whilst reflecting on his work, it is forward looking and challenging, and offers strategies for the future direction of library and information services in the virtual era.

Following an introduction and tribute to Peter on his retirement, the text is contributed by an international team of acknowledged leaders in their fields, and focuses on four key themes that have preoccupied Peter during his career and that remain of pre-eminent importance for the future of the profession:

- libraries, learning and distance learning
- widening access to information
- changing directions of information delivery
- performance, quality and leadership.

The book concludes with a comprehensive bibliography of Peter's work.

This timely book addresses issues and concerns transferable across different areas of the information sector, including academic, public and special libraries, and will be stimulating reading for anyone working, studying, or teaching within the profession.

2008; 256pp; hardback; 978-1-85604-647-3; £44.95

Libraries Without Walls 7

Exploring 'anytime', 'anywhere' delivery of library services

Peter Brophy, Jenny Craven and Margaret Markland, editors

This edited collection is drawn from the seventh Libraries Without Walls Conference, held in 2007. From their beginnings in 1995, the Libraries Without Walls conferences have mapped a major change in the practice of librarianship. While libraries are still concerned to provide users with physical access to their buildings, electronic access – often from remote locations – is becoming ever more dominant, and library services are increasingly being integrated into virtual learning, research and personal environments. In 2007 CERLIM wished to encourage the widest possible range of papers to reflect the diverse current developments in library service delivery. These cover:

- New kinds of service, especially those that open up new paradigms of 'library' – perhaps the library equivalent of YouTube or MySpace.
- The library's role within new models of scholarly publishing, including development of services based on institutional or other repositories, and the responsibility of the library for digital curation.
- Service delivery in challenging environments, especially where the infrastructure may be sub-optimal, as in some developing countries, or where the user group represents particular challenges.
- New technological solutions and the impact on users of the improved services they make possible.
- Delivery and assessment of information skills and literacies, especially where this is achieved through electronic environments.

2008; 264pp; hardback; 978-1-85604-623-7; £44.95

M-libraries

Libraries on the move to provide virtual access

Gill Needham and Mohamed Ally, editors

The development of networked technologies opened up huge opportunities for libraries to make their resources and services accessible to their users regardless of distance. The opportunity to deliver these to users via their mobile phones, PDAs and other handheld devices will be as significant a challenge. Indeed, if libraries choose to ignore this challenge, they are in danger of being left behind in an increasingly competitive world of information provision and services.

This authoritative collection of contributions from experts in the field, based on the First International M-Libraries Conference, explores the technical and social context for m-libraries, describes a range of global initiatives with lessons learned, and discusses the potential for future development. Key areas covered include:

- libraries and net generation learners
- use of mobile technology for off-campus learning
- enhancing access to library resources through mobile communications
- building an effective mobile-friendly digital library
- designing and developing e-learning content for mobile platforms
- architectures and metadata for m-learning and m-teaching
- mobile use and e-learning in developing countries
- from shelf to PDA: transforming mobile devices into LIS tools.

This timely book will be of considerable interest to the growing international mobile learning community across all sectors, not least in developing countries where internet access via computers is poor but many people have mobile phones and other such devices. It should be read not only by information professionals but by mobile, software and library systems suppliers, e-journal suppliers and aggregators, publishers, international development agencies, and policy makers in education and e-government.

2008; 352pp; paperback; 978-1-85604-648-0; £44.95

Digital Consumers
Reshaping the information professions

David Nicholas and Ian Rowlands, editors

The information professions – librarianship, archives, publishing and, to some extent, journalism – have been rocked by the digital transition that has led to disintermediation, easy access and massive information choice. Information now forms a consumer commodity with many diverse information producers engaged in the market.

There is a need for a new belief system that will help information professionals survive and engage in a ubiquitous information environment, where they are no longer the dominant players, nor, indeed, the suppliers of first choice. The aim of this thought-provoking book is to provide that overarching vision, built on hard evidence rather than on PowerPoint 'puff'.An international, cross-sectoral team of contributors has been assembled for this purpose. Key strategic areas covered include:

- the digital consumer: an introduction and philosophy
- the digital information marketplace and its economics: the end of exclusivity
- the e-shopper: the growth of the informed purchaser
- the library in the digital age
- the psychology of the digital information consumer
- the information-seeking behaviour of the digital consumer: case study – the virtual scholar
- the Google generation: myths and realities about young people's digital information behaviour
- trends in digital information consumption and the future.
- where do we go from here?

No information professional or student can afford not to read this far-reaching and important book.

2008; 240pp; hardback; ISBN 978-1-85604-651-0; £39.95

Searching 2.0
Michael P. Sauers

If you aren't intimately familiar with the latest generation of Web 2.0 tools and how to exploit them fully in your daily reference work, then this book is for you. Master trainer Michael Sauers applies the super-search strategies for which he is known to a comprehensive range of tools for reference use, including:

- Web 2.0: definition; core concepts and implications; tagging and folksonomies
- getting organized: bookmarks; web pages; Delicious
- popular search engines: Google; Microsoft's Live Search; Yahoo! Search
- Wikipedia: searching, citing, adding and editing
- searching for media: Flickr; YouTube; Podscope
- local search: Google Maps; Live Search Maps
- print search: Google Book Search; Amazon's 'Search Inside the Book'
- searching the past: The Google Cache; The Wayback Machine; Wikipedia Page Histories
- searching without being there: OpenSearch files; creating OpenSearch plugins
- desktop search: Google Desktop; Windows Search; Windows Vista
- data visualization: Kartoo; Literature Map, etc.

Accessible and fun to read, with a wealth of illustrative screenshots, this is a comprehensive guide to searches that make the most of the Web 2.0 environment. Sauers reviews each Web 2.0 tool for reliability and appropriateness in different search tasks and shows you how best to organize them for quick access at the reference desk.

You (and your users, once you show them how) will use Sauers's advanced and special search methods again and again in your daily reference work. Exercises in each chapter will help you cement your new knowledge into practical reference skills.

March 2009; 350pp; paperback; 978-1-85604-629-9; £44.95

Metadata
Marcia Lei Zeng and Jian Qin

Teachers and trainers seeking a text that covers the theory as well as the practice of metadata application design, implementation, and evaluation will find it in this new, authoritative textbook by internationally recognized metadata experts Zeng and Qin. They have created a comprehensive primer for advanced undergraduate, graduate or continuing education courses on metadata in a range of key areas:

- current standards
- schemas: structure and semantics
- schemas: syntax
- metadata records
- metadata services
- metadata quality measurement and improvement
- achieving interoperability
- the metadata research landscape.

An outcome-based approach allows learners with different orientations to adapt their new knowledge and skills to any electronic domain. Examples and practice problems focus on tasks typical to all metadata application projects.

An ideal classroom tool, this book works equally well for self-guided study. Individual modules can stand alone, for reference on an as-needed basis; when making the transition from traditional cataloguing to compilations of metadata for locally created resources and websites, for example. Or you can study metadata systematically, module by module. Regardless of your approach, this book is the ideal guide to metadata for both students and working information professionals.

2008; 384pp; paperback; 978-1-85604-655-8; £39.95